practicing peace

a devotional walk through the Quaker tradition

c a t h e r i n e   w h i t m i r e   author of *Plain Living*

SORIN BOOKS Notre Dame, Indiana

The Bible quotations used in both the general and chapter introductions are from *The New Oxford Annotated Bible with the Apocrypha, Revised Standard Version*. Reprinted by permission.

The definitions found on pages 269–270 are based on glossaries from the Faith and Practices or Books of Discipline from Mid-America, Ohio Valley, Philadelphia, North Pacific Yearly Meetings of the Religious Society of Friends, and from Janet Hoffman's Testimonies List.

Further copyright acknowledgments may be found on pages 250–254.

© 2007 by Catherine Whitmire

www.sorinbooks.com

ISBN-10 1-933495-07-3   ISBN-13 978-1-933495-07-1

Cover and text design by K. H. Coney

Printed and bound in the United States of America.

Library of Congress Cataloging-in-Publication Data
Whitmire, Catherine.
  Practicing peace : a devotional walk through the Quaker tradition / Catherine Whitmire.
    p. cm.
  Includes bibliographical references.
  ISBN-13: 978-1-933495-07-1 (pbk.)
  ISBN-10: 1-933495-07-3 (pbk.)
  1. Peace--Religious aspects--Society of Friends. 2. Spirituality--Society of Friends. 3. Christian life--Quaker authors. 4. Society of Friends--Doctrines. I. Title.

BX7748.P43W55 2007
248.4'896--dc22

                                        2006033697

For Tom,

Beloved companion on the path to peace

with

love and gratitude

Contents

Preface

Quakers (members of the Religious Society of Friends) have been walking the path to peace for centuries, and the stories of their journeys have much to offer those of us seeking to practice peace today. Since the 1650s, they have been recording their experiences of practicing peace in journals, letters, and articles. There is a long, rich tradition of Quakers individually and collectively reading accounts of one another's spiritual journeys, pondering them, and learning from them. This book attempts to share that tradition.

The quotations included in the main body of chapters 1–6 are all by Quaker authors, and the introductory stories to those chapters include stories about Quakers, regular attenders of Friends meetings, or Quaker institutions. These stories can serve as spiritual guideposts for all those seeking peace. And although these reflections are gleaned from the experiences, thoughts, and prayers of Friends, the process of practicing peace that they describe is universal and accessible to everyone. This book is not about taking "six easy steps to peace." The experiences of Friends suggest that practicing peace is a lifelong, complex, multifaceted spiritual discipline. This book's goal is to offer spiritual accompaniment, encouragement, and guidance for those seeking to practice peace in their personal lives, in their families, and in the wider world.

Another important and long-standing Quaker practice is the use of evocative reflection questions, or *queries*, similar to those found at the end of each section of this book. As used in this text, the queries are intended to engage the reader in personal or group reflection on the spiritual and ethical themes just presented.

A note about inclusive language: Quakerism was born in England at a time when English society was stratified by social class. Quakers, however, believed that the Light of God shone equally in all people, so they would not bow, use honorific titles, or doff their hats. Most notably they insisted on using the grammatically informal "thee" and "thou" when addressing everyone, including the gentry. A contemporary expression of this grammatical adherence to equality is the present-day use by many Friends of gender inclusive language. Therefore I have changed pronouns to be gender inclusive, and have substituted terms such as "the "Commonwealth of God" for the more traditional "Kingdom of God" within quotations.

I must make four brief disclaimers. First, there are several different branches of Quakerism. Although I have included quotations from a wide spectrum of Quaker authors, my selection of these quotations was influenced by my experience as a member of an unprogrammed (silent) meeting in New England.

Second, while the Society of Friends has been practicing peace for over 350 years, there are Quakers who are not committed pacifists. A primary link among most Friends, however, is that we share a heritage of being spiritual pilgrims on a common path to peace.

Third, some of the stories told here have come down to us in letters and journals that did not include the names of the people involved. Therefore, people whose names I do not have are referred to descriptively, for example, "the neighbor" or "the Native American chief."

Finally, when reading selected writings from any group, it may appear that the group is wiser or more virtuous than is their actual practice. In reality, of course, Quaker peacemakers are imperfect people who struggle with feelings of inadequacy, uncertainty, fear, anger, and despair. As Quaker elder John Wilhelm Rowntree once reminded Quakers, "We know better than we do."[1]

Without a strong and sustained spiritual nudge, I would never have written this book. Therefore, in gratitude to the One who nudges me, I am donating all proceeds from *Practicing Peace* to Quaker organizations working for peace and justice.

Gratitudes

I am deeply grateful to the Religious Society of Friends for their peace testimony and for the many Friends, living and dead, whose faith and witness inspired this book.

This compilation of quotations would not have been possible without the interlibrary loan desk at Thomas Memorial Library in Cape Elizabeth, Portland Friends Meeting Library, Friends Meeting at Cambridge Library, Andover Library at Harvard Divinity School, Pendle Hill Library, Haverford College Quaker Collection, Friends Historical Library at Swarthmore College, and Swarthmore College Peace Collection.

Parts of this book were written on retreat and inspired by the peaceable community at Weston Priory, rooted in the tranquility of the Transfiguration Hermitage and wise counsel of Sister Elizabeth Wagner, nurtured by Brother Richard Stanley and others at Eastern Point Retreat House, and sustained by the call of the wilderness at Ring Lake Ranch.

The clearness committee from Portland Friends Meeting that listened prayerfully and encouraged me included Chris Beach, Mary Hillas, and Barbara Potter. Joe and Mary Roy supported me in following my first leading. Carol Becker continues to encourage me to trust my heart. Hugh Barbour gave encouragement and wrote a brief history of Friends peace testimony. Elise Boulding offered resources and provided support, and her vision of a culture of peace inspired much of my work.

I was also inspired by Dorothy Adams, Margaret Hope Bacon, Daniel Barenboim, Charlie Clements, Frances Crowe, Darcy Drayton, Ernie Faust, Lon Fendall, Emma "Hazel" Harrison, Frank Levering, Mary Lord, David Niyonzima, Martha Penzer, Bob Philbrook, David Potorti, Kate Potter, Maria and Tony Reardon, Arthur O. Roberts, Albie Sachs, Wendy Sanford, Skip Schiel, Al Starr, Tom Sturdevant, Marj Swann, Wanda Urbanska, and many others who were willing to share their life stories.

Margaret Hope Bacon also gave historical perspectives and generously suggested stories to research.

I am very appreciative of those who read drafts and offered insights: Jenny Doughty, Brian Drayton, Jonathan Ewell, Zachary Hunter, Noor Johnson, Randy Kehler, Rob Levin, Emily Sander, Brianna Wessel-Estes, Wendy Wickendon, and Greg Williams. Katy Cullinan graciously shared her editorial gifts. Robin Gradison offered helpful and candid analytical perspectives. Ben Schneider submitted invaluable spiritual, organizational, and editorial suggestions.

From Sorin Books: John Kirvan encouraged me to begin this book; Bob Hamma was a gracious reader; and Susana Kelly was a patient, helpful, and professional editor. Parker J. Palmer gave me confidence in my ability to write by doing the foreword for and believing in my first book. I continue to be grateful for his insightful observations and his gracious words.

Margaret Benefiel helped me discern next steps, listened to me read the manuscript, and prayed for me as I wrote. Sharon Daloz Parks helped set me on the path to writing and continues to offer intuitive vision and joyous, loving support. Spirit-friend Emily Sander's empathy, love, wisdom, and creativity continue to illumine my path. Her life is an example of what it means to make love the first motion. My friendships with Margaret, Sharon, and Emily are deep and abiding blessings.

I am thankful for the loving support of my parents, Blanton and Peg Whitmire. I am also grateful that Richard Ewell, Maggie Ewelll, Sarah Ewell, Jonathan Ewell, and Anne Scollins are part of my life. Pam Wessel-Estes's strength, love, creativity, and sense of play deepen my life and I am grateful for the values, integrity, intellectual curiosity, empathy, and spiritual wisdom of my son, Zachary Hunter; his life gives me hope for the future.

My husband, Tom Ewell, is a gifted editor whose insights mark every page. Working on this book together has deepened our relationship. Love is the essence of practicing peace, and Tom's love is a gift from the universe for which I am deeply grateful every day.

Introduction

Quakers have been practicing peace as a spiritual discipline since the 1650s. Their well-worn path to peace begins in prayer and worship, leads to recognizing God in all people, includes practicing nonviolence, and endeavors to make love the guiding force in all they do. This path, which is available to everyone, celebrates life's highest joys and witnesses life's deepest tragedies amidst the beauty, uncertainty, and violence surrounding us. While practicing peace is not always easy, it is a spiritual discipline that expands love, generates hope, and satisfies our soul's deep longing for peace.

My First Steps

I took my own first tentative steps along the path of practicing peace in the manner of Friends at an unlikely time in my life. I was the mother of a preschool-age son and was employed as a health care administrator, feeling overburdened, working long days, and yearning for a more peaceful personal life. It wasn't that I didn't care about the state of the world; there was simply no time for peace work in my already overscheduled days. So, in an attempt to alleviate the stress induced by my busyness, I began meditating every morning and listening within to discern what my next direction in life should be.

As a first step, I was led to simplify my lifestyle, which created more space for meditation, and over time I slowly began to experience more inner peace. However, as I continued to listen within, I grew increasingly spiritually disturbed. Through prayer I was more aware of the world's problems and saw that potential nuclear and biological holocausts were hovering over my son's future. I felt overwhelmed, powerless, and did not know how to educate, prepare, or protect my son in a world filled with so many weapons of mass destruction.

No one had warned me, however, that praying and meditating regularly might change my life in unexpected ways. One morning as I meditated I was surprised by a spiritual nudge to organize a candle-light prayer vigil for peace. I was astonished! I was a new Quaker and had not grown up among peace activists, so I had never attended a prayer vigil, let alone organized one!

I kept praying and listening within, hoping that this spiritual nudge to take action (also called a *leading*) for which I felt so abysmally unprepared, would be lifted from my path. I was already practicing peace through daily meditation, making my family a priority, and working for a nonprofit agency. So why was God asking for more? Soon most of my prayer time was being spent plaintively explaining to God that I was too busy to take on anything else, and pointing out (in case God hadn't noticed) that I was not spiritually prepared or qualified to plan a public prayer vigil.

If truth be told, though, my real motives for resisting this leading were suspect. The thought of holding a candle and praying in public filled me with dread. I was afraid of being embarrassed. What if I looked foolish to people on the sidewalk? I lived in a small town. Would my conservative neighbors stop being friendly? I was afraid of financial repercussions. Would I have to pay a price professionally? Many of my friends were secular and skeptical of prayer. Would they shy away from me for praying in public? I was new at following leadings. If I organized this vigil, what might God ask me to do next? These questions kept arising and I kept procrastinating in the hope that someone else more prepared than I would come forward.

Finally, I began to wonder if perhaps God was reminding me of a prior spiritual commitment. Five years earlier, when I was pregnant, I had watched Golda Meir, Prime Minister of Israel, praying on the evening news that every child born that year be born into a generation of peace. I was living in a house surrounded by tall pines and bordered by a whitewater river. As I listened to her words commingle with the rushing waters and rustling pines, I felt the new life of my child stir in me, and I was flooded with a profound sense of God's compassionate presence. In feeling God's love, I accepted the fact that I was a pacifist and I dedicated myself to trying to make a peaceful world for children everywhere. In that moment of dedication I also experienced a deep sense of promise: God would never leave me alone in my practice of peace. What transpired that evening felt like a private covenant—just between God and me.

Until I felt led to organize the peace vigil nothing out of the ordinary had been required of me. But now my private commitment to God was about to become public. When I finally accepted the fact that my spiritual integrity was hanging on the slim thread of my willingness to make this public witness, I *reluctantly* began organizing. I tentatively shared my leading with friends, who immediately encouraged and supported me in planning the event.

When the day for the vigil arrived I was filled with anxiety, but my fears were unfounded. As I held my candle outside the federal building in a circle with others beneath a soft, gray sky and gently falling snow, I was released from a false sense of social propriety, and I experienced a deep sense of calm.

A picture of our prayer vigil showed up on the front page of the next day's newspaper, and I was surprised and pleased that our message had been acknowledged. But more important to me personally, my relationship with God had been transformed through my reluctant, but faithful spiritual obedience in acting on what I heard while listening within.

Quakerism is sometimes described as an experientially based religion because by acting in faith, Friends often discover what it is they believe.[1] Through my experience of organizing the vigil, I came to believe that God really does lead us through prayer and invites even the unsuspecting, imperfect, and unprepared among us to practice peace.

Meditation and Prayer

Historically for Friends, the path to peace begins (like mine did) with the practice of meditation and prayer. Listening within changes our perspective on the world because when we open ourselves to a prayerful relationship with God, we are invited to view the world from God's perspective. And through God's eyes we see that poverty, violence, and war are not God's choices for the world, but are willful, human decisions.[2]

Over the centuries many people have experienced what educator John Yungblut describes as "an inescapable connection between contemplative prayer and motivation to engage in social reform. It is contemplative prayer that confirms the inseparable unity of all things. It is here that we discover we are not only our brother's and our sister's keeper, but that in some profound sense we *are* our brother and sister."[3] Recognizing our intrinsic oneness deepens our empathy and compassion for others, exposes acts of violence as self-violating, and reveals all wars as civil wars.

Because prayer involves trusting an unseen power and accepting unpredictable results, it is easy to doubt its power and efficacy. Sometimes on snowy evenings, when I am vigiling in prayer lines, and my feet hurt from standing on cold, brick sidewalks, I find myself wondering if our witness is being noticed by passersby and whether our prayers are making a difference. Then I remember the many times I have been introduced as a Quaker and someone says: "Oh, were you one of those people who stood outside in the square in prayer during the Viet Nam (or Panama or Gulf or Afghanistan or Iraq) war? It always renewed my hope to drive by and see you all standing there in witness!" I am then reminded again that in practicing peace through individual and collective meditations and prayers, we gently ruffle the cosmic waters of the world's conscience, generating ripples that affect people's lives in ways that we may never know and creating peaceful outcomes we cannot imagine.

Discernment

Another essential element in Friends' practice of peace is discernment. In prayerful meditation we listen for messages (leadings) from God, and in discernment we try to figure out what those messages mean. If prayer provides us with a nudge to practice peace, discernment helps us know more specifically what God would have us do.

The world's problems loom so large and are so multitudinous that it is easy to feel immobilized and thus unable to address any of them. Discernment, however, helps us see that we are not expected to take on healing the whole world, but only those actions God nudges us and calls us in prayer to undertake.

Personal discernment begins with listening in prayer to discover God's hopes and plans for our lives. Next, it involves sifting prayerfully through what we have heard and trying to separate it from emotions such as fear, pride, and ambition that compromise our judgment. Discernment is not a formula; it is a testing and refining process requiring humility, patience, and prayer.

Learning how to discern God's instruction takes time. There is a story about a man new to Quakerism who was frustrated that he couldn't seem to discern God's messages. He asked the aged and venerable minister, Amos Kenworthy, about the biblical scripture, "My sheep know my voice" (John 10:27). Kenworthy replied, "Yes, it is true that God's sheep know God's voice, but it is also true that the lambs have to learn it."[4]

What we hear in prayer may come as a surprise, so in discernment it is important to stay open to unexpected possibilities. Educator Bill Kreidler wrote that a common response to a message or leading from God is "You want me to do *what*?"[5]

Beyond personal discernment, Friends are also expected to engage in discernment with the community to test the veracity of their prayer leadings. This corporate or communal discernment is central in Friends' decision-making process. Theologian and educator Sharon Daloz Parks describes Quakers as "intra-dependent mystics" because they depend on one another for help in discerning which of their spiritual nudges come from God and which may be arising from ego, anxiety, or self-will.[6] We need one another in discernment because, in the words of the African proverb, "The reason two antelopes walk together is so that one can blow the dust from the other's eyes."[7]

Discernment is a process that also requires ongoing revisiting and monitoring, so even when we think we have discerned God's will for our lives, we still need to keep listening within for continuing guidance. I discovered this years ago when I joined a group of fellow divinity school students who were planning to pray on the grounds of a local industry that made parts for nuclear bombs. After much prayer and discernment, I thought I was clear to join them, even though we would most likely be arrested. I was surprised, because I had never before felt led to civil disobedience. I was also very excited, and felt that I would be doing something heroic to make the world a safer place for children everywhere.

My young son and I discussed what would happen. He would go to our neighbor's house after school, and I would probably be arrested, post bail, and try to be home before he went to bed. However, the night before our action he suddenly looked up at me with big, anxious eyes and said, "Mommy, please don't get arrested." I felt his fear, and heard God speaking through his request. While I was deeply disappointed, it was clear to me that I was not supposed to participate in the civil disobedience part of the protest. This experience taught me that we must *keep* listening within to God's guidance even after we have felt cleared to proceed.

Constructive Anger and Conflict Resolution

Discerning God's will for our lives may sometimes lead us to engage in conflict as we stand up for ourselves and others, speak out for justice, and advocate for peace. And how well we manage our anger in the midst of conflict will determine in large part how successful we will be at resolving our disputes constructively and non-violently. Anger is a God-given emotion that warns us when something is wrong within ourselves, in our personal relationships, or with the world. But when we do not channel our individual and collective angers constructively, they can generate resentments and hostilities that lead to hatred, violence, and warfare.

I began learning about the complexities of displaced, destructive anger as a teenager caught in the intense passions of the 1960s. I was deeply concerned about the civil rights movement, and one morning at the breakfast table after reading about racially motivated violence in the newspaper, I launched into yet another high-volume diatribe against racists. My mother, desperate, no doubt, for some peace and quiet, interrupted me by asking, in words to the effect that, "If you hate people who hate other people, what makes you different from them?"

I replied in a great huff, with all the moral hauteur a sixteen-year-old can muster, "I am *nothing* like those racists in the newspaper!" But, my voice faltered when I said, "Of course I don't *hate* them!" because in my heart of hearts, I knew *I did*. What was even harder to own was that I felt enlivened and emotionally released by the great rushes of red-hot anger generated by my condemnatory tirades. I did not know how to differentiate between individuals and their actions, so I did not understand that it was potentially constructive to be angry about racism, but destructive to hate racists.

My mother's question was troubling. Until that morning I had enjoyed the simple moral clarity of knowing that evil could be easily isolated *outside of me* and located *inside others*. It was so much easier to focus my rage at those I considered prejudiced and hurtful than it was to look within at my own racism and capacity for destructive anger.

I kept wondering about my mother's question: If *my* anger was coming from the same source that fueled *their* violence, did that mean that my anger was also bringing violence and hatred into the world? It would be twenty years before the seed planted by her question would grow into my understanding that destructive anger has no purpose beyond the momentary relief of its own expression and can lead to vengeance, violence, and even war.

Alexander Solzhenitsyn wrote: "If only it were all so simple! If only there were evil people somewhere insidiously committing evil deeds and it were necessary only to separate them. But the dividing line between good and evil cuts through the heart of every human being, and who is willing to destroy a piece of their own heart?"[8] There have never been, and will never be, easy solutions for the problems of evil and violence. But humanity's next step toward renouncing vengeance and laying down violence may be to accept and acknowledge that the dividing line between good and evil does indeed run through each of our hearts.

If we are not careful, prayerful, and nonviolent in our practice of peace, we risk becoming the violence we oppose. The anger and frustration we encounter in working to prevent the proliferation of nuclear weapons, resist budget cuts to the poor, or protect and restore our environment can easily lead us to demonize and even hate those who oppose us. So now when I discover my destructive anger masquerading as moral outrage it helps to remember that Mahatma Gandhi once told people that if they could not find love in their hearts for the British Viceroy, they should not participate in freedom walks such as the Salt March.[9] Mahatma Gandhi, John Woolman, Martin Luther King, Jr., and Desmond Tutu all taught people how to express their anger in loving, nonviolent, and constructive ways because they understood that destructive anger blocks love, breeds hatred, and makes nonviolent conflict resolution and reconciliation difficult, if not impossible.

When we can keep our expressions of anger rooted in love, however, our responses will be nonviolent. There is a Quaker adage about talking with someone in the community whose conduct is upsetting us: "You should not try to elder someone you cannot love."[10]

However, ignoring or denying our anger can also be a source of violence. Repressed or displaced anger has the power to poison relationships, break up communities, and lead to personal, group, and national violence. Counselor Kate Potter describes hidden anger as a stagnant pool of water that festers and breeds disease, while constructively expressed anger runs and splashes over rocks like a bubbling stream, keeping things vibrant and clean as it moves along.[11] Learning how to express our concerns, frustrations, and anger in empathic, nonviolent ways that also clearly state our needs is an important part of practicing peace.

For solving most serious conflicts, our contemporary culture all too often opts for using various forms of violence rather than constructive conflict resolution. Theologian Walter Wink has written at length about why, both as individuals and as nation-states, we so often trust in what he terms the *myth of redemptive violence*:

> Violence is the ethos of our times. It is the spirituality of the modern world. It has been accorded the status of a religion, demanding from its devotees an absolute obedience to death. Its followers are not aware, however, that the devotion they pay to violence is a form of religious piety. Violence is so successful as a myth precisely because it does not seem to be mythic in the least. Violence simply appears to be the nature of things. It is what works. It is inevitable, the last and, often, the first resort in conflicts. It is embraced with equal alacrity by people on the left and on the right, by religious liberals as well as religious conservatives. The threat of violence, it is believed, is alone able to deter aggressors. It secured us forty-five years of a balance of terror. We learned to trust the Bomb to grant us peace. . . .[12]

Violence is "any force that inflicts or threatens harm or injury."[13] And the physical violence dominating daily news reports is only one manifestation of the violence permeating our lives. Teacher Parker J. Palmer writes:

> Violence is done when parents insult children, when teachers demean students, when supervisors treat employees as disposable means to economic ends, when physicians treat patients as objects, when people condemn gays and lesbians "in the name of God," when racists live by the belief that people with a different skin color are less than human. And just as physical violence may lead to bodily death, spiritual violence causes death in other guises—the death of a sense of self, of trust in others, of risk taking on behalf of creativity, of commitment to the common good. If obituaries were written for deaths of this kind, every daily newspaper would be a tome.[14]

Learning to Live Nonviolently

There are now approximately six billion members of the human family, who live in one billion different households, in 189 nation-states, and who are represented in over 10,000 different ethnic groups and communities of various sorts.[15] As our nuclear and biological weapons of mass destruction grow ever more lethal, our swelling populations exponentially increase the possibilities for violent conflicts. We have arrived at a critical moment in history, where our technologies and our numbers make it increasingly risky to rely on our old strategy of trusting bombs and the threat or use of violence to grant us peace. Now is the time to seek new, nonviolent means for resolving our conflicts.

However, we are not destined to suffer endless violence because of our genes, our culture, or history. In 1986 UNESCO (United Nations Educational, Scientific, and Cultural Organization) convened scholars from relevant sciences around the world that released the following statement:

It is scientifically incorrect to say that war or any other violent behavior is genetically programmed into our human nature. While genes are involved at all levels of nervous system function, they provide a developmental potential that can be actualized only in conjunction with the ecological and social environment. While individuals vary in their predispositions to be affected by their experience, it is the interaction between their genetic endowment and conditions of nurturance that determines their personalities. Except for rare pathologies, the genes do not produce individuals necessarily predisposed to violence. Neither do they determine the opposite. While genes are co-involved in establishing our behavioral capacities, they do not by themselves specify the outcome.[16]

This research concludes that we are not predetermined to be violent and gives rise to the expectation that we can, in fact, successfully learn to resolve our conflicts without spiritual, emotional or physical violence. However, we do not come into the world knowing how to live nonviolently. The seeds of nonviolence may lie within each of our hearts, but we have to be awakened to their presence and taught how to cultivate and nurture them. But most of us were never taught how to respond peaceably to the challenges of cultural and racial diversity, how to resolve conflicts creatively, or how to settle personal and international conflicts without resorting to some form of emotional or physical violence. Nonviolence, like any other skill—playing the piano or speaking Spanish—*can* be taught, but it requires learning and practice.

Shortly after I became a Quaker, I was excited to do something to promote nonviolence. So with all the energetic enthusiasm of a novice, I signed up to teach prisoners through the Alternatives to Violence Project (AVP). But it did not occur to me that peace was something I still needed to learn and practice myself. So after volunteering in the prison I was surprised to discover that many of the inmates had been involved with AVP for a long time, and knew more about conflict resolution than I did! I considered myself a pacifist, but I had never been taught how to give "I-statements" effectively, think creatively about confrontation, or look for transforming power in situations of conflict. Learning nonviolence from a group of men, many of them committed to prison for violent crimes, was both humbling and enlightening. My encounters with the AVP-trained prisoners helped me realize that if I wanted to live nonviolently, it was going to take more than good intentions; it was going to involve an ongoing commitment to both learning and practice.

I have also found that I have to *keep* learning and practicing nonviolence, because peace is not a steady state: I find it, lose it, and then have to search for it again. Recently I had the misfortune of being caught in one of Boston's infamous traffic circles during rush hour. It was raining and I was almost hit broadside by a rogue taxi driver who honked loudly for no discernible reason, swore as he passed by, and then abruptly cut in front of me, endangering us both. As he sped off, I was yelling at top volume through the rolled up windows of my car . . . and then I started to laugh! Twenty years and dozens of nonviolence workshops later there I was—still yelling insulting names at a total stranger out of raw anger.

My spontaneous response to a complete stranger who endangered me might be understandable. What is even more disturbing is how quickly my impulse toward judgment, destructive anger, and vengeance can rise when I am in conflict with the people closest to me—my family, friends, and community. In the words of Walter Wink, I am still "a violent person trying to live nonviolently."[17]

Learning how to practice nonviolence is a challenging lifelong journey, and it is therefore important to extend patience and empathy to ourselves whenever we find it difficult or discouraging. When we extend patience and empathy to ourselves we become more accepting of the frailties and lapses of others. So although the potential for violence may always be in us, with God's help, and through conscious efforts to be more empathically self-aware, we *can* grow our hearts into a condition of serenity and peace that counters the inclination toward violence.

Because the potential for violence in ourselves and others is always present, we must be spiritually prepared to encounter it in unexpected moments, and in the most ordinary of places: in our kitchen, when a child repeatedly spills the milk; at our office, when a co-worker becomes verbally abusive; or on our neighborhood sidewalks, when teenagers suddenly lose control.

Some years ago I stopped at the corner market near our house in an economically and ethnically diverse Boston area neighborhood to buy milk for breakfast. As I parked in front of the store, I noticed a group of ten or so young men hanging out on the sidewalk engaged in loud conversation, and I remembered there had been a shooting on this corner a few weeks before. I was reaching for my purse when the voices outside my car suddenly fell quiet, and I heard the sickening thud of boots kicking flesh. The young men had moved up the sidewalk and were now directly beside my car. One of them lay huddled on the ground, while the others kicked him in the stomach and head. He was bleeding. I was less than three feet away. There was no time to formulate an intervention plan. And I was afraid to get involved.

I sat there, temporarily immobilized—until a sudden upwelling of the Spirit lifted me past my fear and nudged me to step out in faith. Remembering from my nonviolence training that surprise is an important element of nonviolent action, I threw open the car door and moved quickly into the circle of angry youths. Shocked by having a middle-aged woman suddenly appear in their midst, they fell back a few steps, and I moved between them and the young man on the ground. I was as surprised to find myself in their circle as they were to have me there!

I immediately began talking with the young men. I never broke eye contact, and every time they started toward me, I took a step toward them and opened my arms wider. This intervention gave the young man on the ground the opportunity to limp to a nearby house for help, and the others soon dispersed.

As I stood in the circle, I saw that the perpetrators were all around my son's age. My heart opened, and I was able to love them as if they were my sons, which, on a deeper level, of course, they were. Seeing with the eyes of my heart allowed concern, empathy, and love to rise up in me both for the bloodied young man on the ground, and for the young men standing on the pavement, who, unlike my son, would most likely never attend college, and who were angry and desperate enough about their lives to resort to this kind of violence.

Nonviolence is love in action. It was the power of a Loving Presence beyond myself that pushed me into that circle of teenagers. To this day, I have no idea what I said to them—but I don't think my words made any difference. I believe the young men on the sidewalk stopped their violence because they felt me trying to mediate God's love to them. This episode helped me understand nonviolence as a process of co-creation, of receiving God's love into our hearts and trying to embody it in our lives. As I stood facing the teenagers sullenly clenching their fists, I was surprised to find that I did not feel alone, so I was not immobilized by fear.

Eighteen years earlier when I was pregnant in the house beside the river, I experienced a reassuring sense of promise that I would never be left by myself when witnessing for peace. That was a promise kept—I was not alone on the sidewalk with the angry teenagers. God's presence was with me in the accumulated power of every prayer I had ever said, every worship service I had ever attended, and every act of love and compassion I had ever given or received.

During this encounter I employed many of the common elements of nonviolence: a sense of God nudging me to act, discernment to act quickly, nonviolence training, a creative response, and a loving acceptance of those involved. This episode also involved recognizing the essential goodness in each person, and reaching out in unexpected ways that shifted the moral ground, throwing the aggressors off-balance and creating space for a nonviolent resolution to emerge.

The practice of nonviolence, of course, is not always successful in addressing violent behaviors or oppressions. But I believe that acts of violence are *never* successful in bringing about true justice or peace. History reveals that violence sows seeds of vengeance that in turn take root and initiate new cycles of violence. While nonviolent actions leave no need for vengeful reprisals and have the power to mediate love, transform hearts, and restore relationships.

Love

Our capacity to love the difficult parts of ourselves and others is the foundation upon which our practice of peace is built. But love is never easy and requires of us an ongoing willingness to be challenged, broken open, and changed.

Some years ago, my husband and I were visiting Midcoast Meeting in Maine when an older couple, Maria and Tony Reardon, beloved to each other and the meeting, were celebrating their fiftieth wedding anniversary. Maria rose during the silent worship, placed her hand on her husband's shoulder, looked down at him tenderly, and shared with the meeting how much she loved him. Then she lifted her head, looked out at those assembled and gently mused aloud, "You know, love at any age takes everything you've got."[18]

Love does take everything we've got, but it is also the primary power we have to transform the escalating violence of these times. Martin Luther King, Jr., said that "violence is a descending spiral, begetting the very thing it seeks to destroy . . . adding deeper darkness to a night already devoid of stars. Darkness cannot drive out darkness; only light can do that. Hate cannot drive out hate; only love can do that."[19]

All too often, however, God's laws about loving one another are overridden by secular laws that cause human suffering, abuse the environment, or generate vengeance.[20] Corporate excesses that deplete resources intended for the common good; social policies that neglect the poorest of the poor; legislative mandates that allow or condone fouling our air, land, and water; and prisoner abuse tantamount to torture may all be tolerated within secular law, but they are violent and stand in opposition to God's laws of love.

Getting through this difficult portal in history will require of each of us all the love we can individually and collectively generate. So it is up to us to love ourselves, each other, and the earth as best we can. In 1693 William Penn wrote:

> Let us then try what love will do. . . .
> Love is the hardest lesson in Christianity,
> but for that reason it should be most our care to learn it.[21]

Envisioning

The ancient desire for peace is deeply embedded in human hearts. Peace researcher Elise Boulding has found that as far back as we have written records, there are myths and legends about people envisioning "peaceable gardens."[22] She writes:

> It is great comfort to me, when I get discouraged about the
> state of humanity, to realize that every civilizational tradition,
> no matter how warlike or materialistic its history, contains in
> its literary record imagery concerning a Peaceable Garden.
> The Peaceable Garden is a public space, often a garden or
> green meadow, where people have laid aside weapons and live
> together in peace: feasting, playing, talking philosophy, and
> reciting poetry. The Greeks knew it, the desert Bedouin knew
> it. We have an enduring capacity to visualize humans as better
> than we experience ourselves to be and the social order as
> more harmonious than what we see around us.[23]

A central vision of peace in the gospel is that of the Commonwealth (traditionally called Kingdom) of God. Jesus refers repeatedly to this peaceable Commonwealth as being near and even says that it lies within us.[24] Most of us have already experienced the immediate presence and peace of God's Commonwealth at the most human and personal level when holding a newborn child, watching a seed sprout from the earth, or looking into the calm immensity of a starry sky. In addition to our personal experiences in families, neighborhoods, and communities, we are aware of that peaceable Commonwealth when responding to a neighbor's call for help, receiving consolation from a friend, supporting a colleague, or settling a serious disagreement through open and loving dialogue. Economist and peace educator Kenneth E. Boulding says that he knows the peaceable Commonwealth of God on earth is possible, because he has experienced it. And he reminds us that: "What exists is possible!"[25]

Jesus says that while this Commonwealth is present now, it is also part of the future and still needs to be built.[26] *So the paradoxical truth of the peaceable Commonwealth of God is that it is both here now—and it is our life's work to create it!*

A number of years ago, after working hard against the latest war, I was physically weary, emotionally drained, and spiritually exhausted after years of always being against the social evils of poverty, violence, and warfare. Intrepid activist Peace Pilgrim wrote, "You have much more power when you are working for the right thing than when you are working against the wrong thing. And, of course, if the right thing is established wrong things will fade away of their own accord."[27] While working against policies that create suffering and kindle violence is important, working for visions that bring peace has special power.

I wanted to feel truly alive, and I was tired of waiting for others to create the culture of peace I had been envisioning. So I decided to try living *as if* it had already arrived by living differently. I moved into an economically and racially diverse neighborhood where my son played with children from different countries and attended public schools with a kindergarten through high school peace curriculum. I also expanded my garden, opened our home for community singing parties, took more walks with friends, and created annual celebrations with neighbors such as welcoming the first flower each spring. And as I began living the more peaceable life I had envisioned, I started to feel physically restored, emotionally rested, spiritually re-centered, and renewed in my commitment to work for peace. I also kept discerning and letting go of extraneous activities, so, over time, even though I was working, I found I was better able to focus on my prayer life, spend more time with my family, and work with my faith community.

I was re-energized, because I felt that I was just where God wanted me to be. I had been waiting for peace to arrive, but what I discovered is that it is more likely to appear when we begin living it. Peace activist Emily Green Balch once reflected, "There is no way to peace; peace is the way."[28]

Children yet to be born are depending on us to envision the peaceable Commonwealth and to work toward making it a future reality. So, from time to time I close my eyes, open my heart, and imagine a hundred years into the future. I picture my great-great-grandchildren running home from school through a sun-dappled meadow in a safe and beautiful urban park, breathing good air and pausing to drink clean water from a public fountain. The schools they attend are teaching peacemaking and conflict resolution skills to children from diverse racial and ethnic groups. They are learning in their history classes that it was only fifty years ago that the world banned nuclear weapons, cancelled the debt of poor nations, passed strong environmental laws, and declared food, water, shelter, education, and healthcare to be basic human rights.

As I relax into my peaceful visions of what was achieved by what educator Joanna Macy calls "the great turning" of the twenty-first century, my heartbeat slows and my shoulders loosen as my anxieties about the future are soothed.[29] I am filled with a deep sense of inner peace.

Elise Boulding invites us to tend our visions by beginning to envision peace today!

> We can't work for something we can't imagine! We urgently need, individually, in our families . . . and in all the groups we work with, to spend significant periods of time in deep reflection about—and envisioning of—an earth-world that has become the peaceable garden it was created to be. A more local earth-world, in which all living things are attuned to one another and learn from one another. A world full of music, and the joy of work, and the joy of play. Our vision will empower our action as each of us begins to use the tools we have, in the settings in which we move, in ways that will tend and sustain the peaceable garden. We are all gardeners, and the vision is the journey.[30]

When we plant our visions deep in the "furrows of the world's pain" and cultivate them by practicing peace, we *can* grow peaceful and compassionate possibilities for our children's futures.[31]

This envisioning is not just wishful thinking. In my lifetime Jim Crow laws were dismantled, women received the right to become judges and astronauts, the Berlin wall fell, and Apartheid crumbled. Also 3.4 billion people, or 64 percent of the world's population, including India, Czechoslovakia, Philippines, Russia, South Africa, and the Ukraine changed governments without going to war.[32] Humanity can and does change. *We have reason to believe that a world without war is possible.*

Standing in the Gaps

In the meantime we are faced with the problem of living in the challenging and often precarious gap between the way things *are* and the way they *could be*. Parker J. Palmer said: "There is no easy solution. There never has been and never will be. But we must learn to stand in this gap, faithfully holding the tension and negotiating between what is and what is possible."[33]

Over the centuries Quakers have responded as best they could to God's call to stand in the gaps. Through their faithful, but imperfect, obedience to God's summons, they became involved in challenging religious intolerance, the injustices of slavery, the lack of women's rights, and the tragedy of war. They did not set out to change the world, but the world did, in fact, change as a result of their willingness to stand in the gaps.

Through prayer and discernment we, too, can know in which gaps God would have us stand. Our efforts may feel unimportant, but nothing is too small to make a difference.[34] We may be led to write a peace poem, grow vegetables, raise children, drive hot meals to the elderly, save turtles in a wetland, teach refugees to read, or educate ourselves about racism. Or we may be called to organize prayer vigils for peace, offer nonviolence trainings in prisons, protest against torture, or join an international peace team. Our tools may include organic seeds, compost piles, guitars, birthday cards, e-mail lists, and peace banners. We may be sustained by hot cups of tea, locally grown strawberries, new songs, old and abiding friendships, and deep worship.[35] However, when we live with kindness, work with patience, and make love the first motion in all we do, peace will follow us wherever we go.

It may be tempting to try to avoid the uncertainty and difficulty of living in the gaps, but as Joshua Rowntree wrote in 1913, "Who knoweth whether we are not come to the commonwealth for such a time as this?"[36] While we may feel inadequate, unprepared, or fearful to go into the gaps, God is undeterred by our trepidation. God asks: "Who shall ascend the hill of the Lord? And who shall stand in God's holy place?"[37] It is important that we climb God's holy hill and stand in the social, political, and spiritual gaps of our times, not only because God calls us, but because there is no one else to go. Thomas R. Kelly wrote:

> No giant figure of heroic size will stalk across the stage of history today, as a new Messiah. But in simple, humble, imperfect people like you and me wells up the spring of hope. We

have this treasure of the seed in earthen vessels—very earthen vessels. You and I know how imperfect we are. Yet those little demonstrations of love and goodwill . . . deeds done in the midst of suffering . . . stir hope that humanity as a whole will be aroused to yield to the press and surge of the Eternal Love within them. . . .[38]

It is *our* turn now to stand watch through the night. If we listen carefully we may hear God entreating us to come up—prepared or not—to stand in the gaps, holding our children, singing our songs, calling for justice, and offering beams of hope by letting our lives reflect what the power of Love can do.

Blessings on your journey!

Chapter 1

Practicing Peace with Ourselves through

Loving Ourselves

Spiritual Renewal

Prayer and Worship

Leadings and Discernment

Faith

Practicing Peace with Ourselves through Loving Ourselves

"You shall love the Lord your God with all your heart, and with all your soul, and with all your mind, and with all your strength. The second is this, You shall love your neighbor as yourself. There is no other commandment greater than these."

Mark 12:30–31

In the late 1990s, a group of New England women gathered seasonally at a retreat house on the rocky coast of Massachusetts to worship and share their personal celebrations and struggles. One year during an early spring retreat, Wendy Sanford, a widely respected writer and editor, told the group that she had been worried and anxious about how to address debilitating conflicts within a cooperative writing project where she had a leadership role. To help herself deal with this anxiety, Wendy shared that she had started praying the prayer attributed to Saint Francis: "Lord, make me an instrument of your peace. . . ." What came back to her from that prayer "was the sudden realization that God knew before giving me this piece of work that I am an instrument who gets anxious." Wendy Sanford said that once she recognized and accepted God's confidence in her gifts, her anxiety lifted, and she was better able to address the conflicts within the writing project.[1]

God loves us, understands our struggles, and calls us to love ourselves for who we are—imperfect but precious instruments of peace. How easy it is to forget that the precondition of loving our neighbor, as suggested in Mark 12, is that we *first* must love ourselves. Perhaps remembering to practice self-love is difficult because we know our humanness all too well: the fears we justify as prudent, the insecurities we quietly nurse, and the anxieties that immobilize us and keep us from living fully into our gifts. God, however, is invested in our loving ourselves, because when we do, we become more accepting of others and are better able to employ our talents as instruments of peace on behalf of the common good.

Our capacity to love our neighbor is diminished because we don't do such a good job of loving ourselves. . . . As we look at the task of peacemaking in these times when the war drums are beating so loud and the potential for bad news is so fierce, we want to be absolutely careful . . . and gentle with ourselves and sometimes this is a concept that is very difficult. Maybe we didn't grow up learning it at home. But, I would like to suggest to you that the more mercy that you have for yourself, the more mercy you will have for the next person. The more patience and tolerance that you have for the aspects of yourself for which you are not comfortable, the more patience you are going to have for the next person.

John Calvi, 2003

. . . It is somehow easier, at least for me, to accept that others are the daughters and sons of God than that I am. When others are unkind, foolish or downright bad we can make excuses for them—they were worried, ill-informed, had an unhappy childhood, were under strain, etc. Where we ourselves are concerned, however, we are all too aware of the trivial thoughts, the dubious motives, the laziness, vanity, greed and so on. How can we believe in that of God in ourselves? What shred of evidence have we?

Adam Curle, 1981

"Inasmuch as ye have done it unto one of the least of these my people, ye have done it unto me." At the beginning, it might be well to note that this responsibility to accept all [people] has a very difficult catch in it. It might even apply to self-acceptance.

practicing peace

The psychologist Jung has most disconcertingly asked whether one of "the least of these" . . . might possibly be my own despised self whom I am forever bemoaning as too heavy a burden to bear, or bitterly reproaching Providence for not having made me more handsome, or more brilliant, or more capable, or more attractive. Dom Chapman once suggested in a letter to a friend that "it is really a very perfect act of love to God" to accept ourselves and to put this scarred and wearisome person into God's hands and get on with the work to be done.

Douglas Steere, 1966

It is by our "imperfections"
that we move towards each other,
towards wholeness of relationship.
It is our oddities, our grittiness,
the occasions when we hurt or are hurt,
that challenge us to a deeper knowledge of each other.
Our sins have been said to be stepping stones to God.

Kenneth C. Barnes, 1985

We are clumsy, we are partial, we are wounded—
and you and I are enough.
You are enough to be fully faithful.
You are enough,
and God affirms you.

Jan Wood, 2003

And thou,
faithful babe,
though thou stutter and stammer forth
a few words in the dread of the Lord,
they are accepted.

William Dewsbury, 1660

There in my God's world all potentials glowed as possibilities. Here on my sentry duty in the actual world I see them stained, bungled and botched by my inability to let God's music play on all the strings of my being, while I at most can make a single life-thread throb, which I can express in action. And in spite of this suffering, due to my own limitation, I must act, I must let all rich potential be absorbed in some single real creative act. For woe is me if this is not done.

Emilia Fogelklou, 1911

I want to be fully myself,
the person that I was created to be,
because the full flowering of myself
is what the world most needs.

Mary Louisa Gray, 2001

Our need to accept ourselves as a whole, and offer that whole to God, leaving it to God "unto whom all hearts are open, all desires known, and from whom no secrets are hid" to evaluate the good and bad in us. The glorious miracle is that, if we can do this, God can still use us, with all our faults and weaknesses, if we are willing to be used.

Anna Bidder, 1978

Remember then thy station as being sacred to God.
Accept of the strength freely offered to thee. . . .

John Woolman, 1764

The peace and justice for which we long do not depend on our goodness, strength or wisdom. The Good News is that God, who already knew our weakness even before we confessed it, chooses—even so—to use us from time to time to give expressions to the peace and justice which are at the very heart of God.

Ben Richmond, 2003

Queries

What do I cherish about myself? What do I believe God and others cherish about me? Are they the same?

In what ways do my concerns about my limitations keep me from being an instrument of peace?

In what ways have my imperfections been stepping stones to God? To others?

Practicing Peace with Ourselves
through Spiritual Renewal

God is my shepherd, I shall not want; God
makes me lie down in green pastures. God leads
me beside still waters; God restores my soul. God
leads me in paths of righteousness for God's
name sake. Even though I walk through the
valley of the shadow of death, I fear no evil, for
thou art with me; thy rod and thy staff, they
comfort me.

Psalm 23:1–4

Bayard Rustin, chief organizer of Martin Luther King, Jr.'s March on Washington, D.C., once spent a weekend in New York City doing political canvassing. He was with a group of social activists working in the Lower East Side where tall tenements loomed over narrow streets, filtering out most of the sunlight and darkening the debris-littered sidewalks. His canvassing partner for the weekend said that for the first hours or so he had a difficult time following Bayard because he was erratic in his canvassing, changing sides of the street and pausing at almost every intersection. After a while, his canvassing partner recognized the pattern: Bayard walked only on the sunlit side of the street and lingered for a few moments on each corner where he took pleasure in lifting his face toward the sun. After observing Bayard finding enjoyment in difficult circumstances, his canvassing partner concluded that Bayard had the strength to survive the abuse and jail sentences he endured as a civil rights organizer, in large part because he so deeply cherished the gift of life.[2] Bayard Rustin knew to keep looking towards that renewing Spirit which forever shines above the bleakness and despair of the ghetto and the jail cell.[3]

Author E.B. White mused, "I arise in the morning torn between a desire to *save* the world and a desire to *savor* the world. This makes it hard to plan the day."[4] However, God encourages us to find a balance in our daily lives between saving and savoring the world. These are not opposite choices, but are part of God's plan whereby spiritual renewal inspires us to both enjoy God's creation and work to restore it to peace and wholeness.

Looking down at sin, and corruption, and distraction,
you are swallowed up in it;
but looking at the Light that discovers them,
you will see over them.
That will give victory;
and you will find grace and strength and there is the first step of
     peace.

George Fox, 1658

. . . When your faith doesn't bring you
the peace that passeth all understanding,
when it doesn't bring you joy,
when it allows no rest for the weary,
there's something wrong. . . .
Do we trust in our own hands more than in the One who guides
     them?
Do we think we can create the Commonwealth of God in the world
when it does not reside in our own hearts?

Kat Griffith, 2005

Sabbath is God's gift to a tired soul. . . .
The world aches to be ministered to
by people who are well-rested,
people who have lain still long enough

to let the grace and peace of God settle on them.
God wants us to be a well-rested people.

Brad Tricola, 2005

[Perspective] can only be rediscovered
by our willingness to recognize
that there is a natural balance between work and rest,
and that the constant striving for perfection is
probably the surest way of missing the mark altogether.
We have to recognize that there is an inbuilt rhythm in life
to which we need to adjust so that we can respond to its ebb and
    flow.
Such a recognition and adjustment
will come about as we stop and stand still in silence. . . .

George H. Gorman, 1973

It isn't easy to stop. Sometimes we suffer intense pangs from our
compulsive nature when we step out of the whirlwind. It can be
helpful to realize that the pain has been there all along, because of
the way we've been living; we're just letting ourselves feel it at
last. But God's mercy will sustain us in that inward retirement.

Douglas Gwyn, 1996

. . . I read 1 Kings 19:3–8 about Elijah and found he was running
for his life under a death threat when he went into the wilderness.
Does he find the tempter there? Does he pray for God to be with
him? No. He prays he might die, then promptly falls asleep, hoping never to wake again.

However, he is awakened by an angel who says, "Arise and eat,"
and there is a cake (baked, even!) and a jug of water. So he eats
and falls asleep again, and again an angel wakes him to tell him
not only to eat, but to journey from there in God's strength.
"And he went in the strength of that food forty days and forty
nights as far as Horeb, the mountain of God." It is there (after

the earthquake, wind, and fire) that Elijah hears the still small voice of God giving instructions for his next call: go back into the wilderness, anoint kings in Syria and Israel and anoint Elisha to succeed you as prophet. For Elijah, a time of rest in the wilderness was necessary to prepare him for hearing God's voice anew.

. . . From Elijah's story, I learn if we find ourselves in a wilderness feeling separated from God by our own sense of inadequacy or fear, it may be we need to listen for the angel who says, "Arise and eat." After eating and sleeping as God leads, this spiritual rest and food will carry us during the long journey to the place where God will reveal God's self to us anew and send us on to new ministries.

Janet Hoffman, 2001

Solitude is a gift of time without accompanying distraction,
an opportunity to keep company with one's own soul.
It is where the Spirit can help one
harness one's own cross in such a way that
it can be carried without too great strain

John Yungblut, 1990

True silence . . .
is to the spirit
what sleep is to the body,
nourishment and refreshment.

William Penn, 1699

One of the striking facts in the Old Testament
is how often the ideas of stillness and strength occur together.
Probably the best-known passage is Isaiah 40:31. . . .
"Those who wait on the Lord will renew their strength.
They will soar on wings like eagles;
they will run and not grow weary,
they will walk and not tire."

Howard R. Macy, 1988

I have found that the more I enjoy living—
the more I learn to lift up my heart—
the easier it is to accept life cheerfully,
because it means living from the deep joy of inward peace.
But the price is to feel the pain of the world more acutely.
But if we live in the flow of balanced inbreath and outbreath
nothing is too difficult.

Margaret E. Wilkinson, 1978

. . . I find it right and helpful to create parks in our crowded and
over populated minds—times or occasions in which we seek and
find escape. This kind of escape I am sure is right, compatible
with unflinching realistic knowledge of all that is disturbing. Do
you remember Robert Louis Stevenson's story of a hard fighting
old Huguenot dying in murderous religious warring, saying, "My
mind is like a garden, full of fountains and shelters." . . . So I
hope you will find and use enough shelters and fountains to give
you what you need.

Emily Green Balch, undated letter, ca. 1943

There is a river,
a sweet, still flowing river,
the streams whereof will make glad thy heart.
And learn but in quietness and stillness to retire to God,
and wait upon the Spirit;
in whom thou shalt feel peace and joy,
in the midst of thy troubles from the cruel and vexatious spirit of
    this world.

Isaac Penington, 1675

So the Lord God Almighty of power and life and wisdom,
keep you and preserve you all . . .
that you may be abundantly refreshed in the One,
who is full of grace, of truth,
that of God's truth you may receive grace for grace. . . .

And that you may abide in God,
and God's word abide in you,
that you may bring forth much fruit. . . .

Margaret Fell, 1658

Drop thy still dews of quietness,
Till all our strivings cease:
Take from our souls the strain and stress,
And let our ordered lives confess
the beauty of thy peace.
Breathe through the heats of our desire
Thy coolness and thy balm
Let sense be dumb, let flesh retire;
Speak through the earthquake,
Wind, and fire,
O still, small voice of calm.

John Greenleaf Whittier, 1872

Queries

In my daily life, how am I balancing my need to both save and savor the world? In what ways does savoring the world help renew both my soul and my practice of peace?

How do I monitor the status of my body, mind, and soul so that I know when it is time to rest and renew myself?

What do I do to renew my body? My soul? Do I have regular times for spaciousness, solitude, silence, and rest in my daily, weekly, monthly, and yearly routines?

Practicing Peace with Ourselves
through Prayer and Worship

Rejoice in your hope,
be patient in tribulation,
be constant in prayer.

Romans 12:12

On a cold January day in 1817, Elizabeth Fry, wife of a merchant and mother of ten children, made her first visit to female inmates at the infamous Newgate prison in London. Elizabeth felt called to visit prisoners by her own prayer and by the prayerful encouragement of others, but her gentle background made her an unlikely candidate for this service. The jailors were reluctant to admit her and explained that the women prisoners she wanted to visit often attacked and tore the clothes from those who entered their large common yard. Elizabeth listened politely to the guards' dire warnings, and then quietly asked to be admitted.

The dungeon was gloomy and rank, and the din of shrieks was almost deafening. But when the crowd of rough women surged toward Elizabeth, the jailors were shocked to see that they did not attack her. They recognized her plain Quaker dress and bonnet as religious garb, and when she calmly said that she had come as a mother, distressed for them and their children, their hearts were touched, and they refrained from violence.[5]

Led by prayer, Elizabeth started the Association for the Improvement of the Female Prisoner in Newgate, whereby women from outside the prison volunteered to take turns comforting, feeding, clothing, and praying with the inmates. They also taught the prisoners sewing, reading, and employment skills. Their empowerment work with the inmates was so successful that city authorities eventually began to adopt the Association's humane approach and practices in other prisons. Elizabeth went on to spark a worldwide prison reform movement by speaking about the deplorable plight of prisoners, first to the English House of Commons, and eventually to kings and government representatives across Europe.[6]

Elizabeth did not set out to become a prison reformer. Her prayers, and the prayers of others, drew her into this unexpected role. While prayer is often comforting and healing, it can also be a powerful and compelling practice that leads us down unanticipated paths. The word *prayer* rises from the same Latin root as the word *precarious*.[7] Author Annie Dillard wrote about the dynamic, uncertain nature of prayer: "It is madness to wear ladies straw hats and velvet hats to church; we should all be wearing crash helmets. Ushers should issue life preservers and signal flares; they should lash us to our pews. For the sleeping god may wake someday and take offense or the waking god may draw us out to where we can never return."[8] Prayer can, as it did for Elizabeth Fry, lead us out to precarious edges where God opens our hearts and transforms our lives in unexpected ways.

I often wonder if we really know how dangerous meeting for worship is. By making ourselves totally open to the working of the Spirit, by reaching down beyond our deepest selves to the very ground of our being, who knows what may happen? We are in effect offering a blank check of our lives. This may lead us in directions we had never dreamed of, to new challenges and new ways of living adventurously. Those who think that worship in meeting will give them a quiet life may be in for a surprise. It is this kind of prayer that breaks us out of the cycle of apathy, despair and helplessness, to acts of prophetic resistance we never knew we were capable of.

Helen Steven, 2005

A F/friend and elder I know who is an historian . . . said, "Early Friends went to Meeting expecting to be changed." [They] expected to be changed every time they met. Every time! They reminded us about being willing to wrestle with God. Remember that Jacob was changed by that experience. Early Friends wrestled with God minute by minute, second by second, breath by breath.

Deborah Fisch, 2003

To pray is to change.
Prayer is the central avenue God uses to transform us.
If we are unwilling to change,
we will abandon prayer as a noticeable characteristic of our lives. . . .

Richard J. Foster, 1978

When I give workshops, I often go around the room and ask people to give a reason they have for not praying. This is actually pretty easy for folks. They usually respond by saying, "I don't have enough time." Or "I don't know how to pray." Or "I am not sure God answers prayers." But I will never forget the woman who said, "I am afraid of what God will ask me to do." And I thought, "You know, that is a darn good reason to not pray." Because it implies that you know the power of prayer. . . .

Whenever the angels appear in scripture, the first thing they say is "Fear not." They say "Fear not," but we are afraid, and we have every right to be. To be used and changed by the Creator is a fearsome thing.

Bill Kreidler, 1994

I was given [a] lesson in prayer by a grandmother whose life read like the Book of Job. . . . One day I asked her how she could be so strong and at peace. She replied that her grandmother told her, "Now honey, when you pray don't ask God to take away your troubles. Just ask God to make your shoulders strong enough to carry them." I'm learning to pray as she did for the strength and faith to accept all that I can't understand and don't want to carry.

Mary Ann Downey, 2003

God is our refuge and strength, a very present help in trouble (Psalm 46:1). . . . A modern paraphrase of this verse might be: "God is our instant help when we are in a tight squeeze." . . . But there is a condition to receive God's presence—it can only be immediately available if we ask. So in the middle of feeling squeezed, we have to train our minds and hearts to remember to call out and ask for God's help. Rather than succumbing to the load and our feelings of weakness, God gives us the remedy—Be still, and know that I am God (Psalm 46:10).

Trish Edwards-Konic, 2003

. . . It is good to spend some time in a wordless, un-striving sense of the presence of God, in which my only purposeful act is to direct my attention towards someone I wish to pray for. Sitting in the light, I see the person in that Light, and in a sense I just stand together with him or her in the Presence.

Brian Drayton, 2006

In the practice of group worship on the basis of silence come special times when the electric hush and solemnity and depth of power steals over the worshipers. A blanket of divine covering comes over the room, a stillness that can be felt is over all, and the worshipers are gathered into a unity and synthesis of life, which is amazing indeed. A quickening Presence pervades us, breaking down some part of the special privacy and isolation of our individual lives and blending our spirits within a superindividual Life and Power. An objective, dynamic Presence enfolds us all, nourishes our souls, speaks glad, unutterable comfort within us, and quickens us in depths that had before been slumbering. The Burning Bush has been kindled in our midst, and we stand together on holy ground.

Thomas R. Kelly, 1940

The most essential preliminary to peacemaking is prayer, or meditation.

Adam Curle, 1981

practicing peace

If contemplation, which introduces us to the very heart of creation,
    does not inflame us with such love that it gives us,
together with deep joy,
the understanding of the infinite misery of the world,
it is a vain kind of contemplation;
it is the contemplation of a false God.
The sign of true contemplation is charity.

Marius Grout, ca. 1945

True godliness does not turn people out of the world,
But enables them to live better in it,
And excites their endeavors to mend it. . . .

William Penn, 1682

To the extent that our peace witness and work
are separate from the life of the Spirit,
we lose the power to effect change in the world.

Bruce Birchard, 2004

I ask for daily bread, but not for wealth, lest I forget the poor.
I ask for strength, but not for power, lest I despise the meek.
I ask for wisdom, but not for learning, lest I scorn the simple.

I ask for a clean name, but not for fame, lest I condemn the lowly.
I ask for peace of mind, but not for idle hours, lest I fail to hearken to the call of duty.

Inazo Nitobe, 1909

Heavenly Father, heavenly Mother,
Holy and blessed is your true name.
We pray for your reign of peace to come,
We pray that your good will be done,
Let heaven and earth become one.
Give us this day the bread we need,
Give it to those who have none.

Let forgiveness flow like a river between us,
From each one to each one to each one.
Lead us to holy innocence
Beyond the evil of our days—
Come swiftly Mother, Father, come.
For yours is the power and the glory and the mercy:
Forever your name is All in One.

Parker J. Palmer, 1992

Gentle spirit, Immanuel. . . .
Open within us understanding of the parables in our own lives.
Lead us as a faith community to minister to one another.
Help us to develop programs where we can learn and practice
the skills needed to be peacemakers in today's world.
And as you scatter us to the winds of the world
continue to heal us and to feed us with your life
that we may listen deeply to other people.
Help us to serve you in all that we do.

Judy Brutz, 1986

Queries

How, when, and where do I pray? Does my prayer include at least as much listening as talking?[9]

Do I enter into prayer and worship honestly, openly, and expecting to be changed? Do I watch for the "coincidences" that happen when I pray?

When has prayer unexpectedly transformed my life or the life of someone I know?

Practicing Peace with Ourselves
through Leadings and Discernment

Behold,
I stand at the door
and knock. . . .

Revelation 3:20

New Hampshire schoolteacher Darcy Drayton received a surprising leading in 2002 while attending a conference in Kenya. After an exhausting day visiting Friends programs in the slums of Nairobi, she was meditating during evening prayers in her hotel room when she suddenly experienced a strong spiritual nudge to go back downstairs and talk to the waiter who had earlier served her a ginger ale at the hotel's outside restaurant. In Darcy's words:

> Though I am outgoing by nature, it does not necessarily make it easier to obey a command like this from God. I, a mzungu [white person], going down to tell a native waiter . . . what? That God told me to go talk to him?! It was already late; I was tired; I didn't really want to do this, but I did. . . . The staff was finishing up their evening shift. I found my waiter. I told him that he might think what I had to say to him was strange, that I had been praying and felt that God wanted me to come down and talk to him.[10]

In the course of their short conversation she told the waiter, whose name was Jairus, about her visit that day to the Lindi Friends School, which serves AIDS orphans of all tribes and is located in the desperately poor and dangerous Kibera slums. Darcy told Jairus that she planned to return to the school the next day, and he expressed an interest in meeting her there.

The following day Jairus did join Darcy briefly at the school. Over time Darcy discovered that Jairus had grown up Quaker, and had attended a Quaker school in western Kenya, but that he had not been to a Friends Meeting for some years.

Darcy's faithful discernment of what she heard in prayer and her willingness to follow her leading changed both their lives. As a result of their meeting, Darcy learned that Jairus eventually joined the Quaker Meeting in Nairobi. And Darcy, deeply moved by her encounter with Jairus and inspired by a sense that she was being led by God into action, began raising money for the Lindi Friends School, writing about poverty in Kenya, and working to raise awareness of the impact of AIDS in Africa.[11] Darcy writes: "In modern life it is hard to believe that miracles can happen or that God can speak prophetically through us. This was not the burning bush of Moses. Yet it was a leading and I followed it."[12]

When we listen within for the one who knocks and faithfully act on what we hear, we never know where we will be led or how taking action may change our life and the lives of those around us.

If God ever spoke
God is still speaking.
If God has ever been in mutual and reciprocal communication
with the persons God has made,
God is still a communicating God
as eager as ever to have listening and receptive souls.
If there is something of God's image and superscription
in our inmost structure and being,
we ought to expect a continuous revelation
of God's will and purpose through the ages. . . .
God is the *Great I am*,
not a Great I Was.

Rufus M. Jones, 1948

The witness of the Society of Friends has always been in the fact that the apostolic period of the Christian witness has never stopped; that the epoch of the Holy Spirit is upon us; and that the revelation of the power of the Spirit, which the Book of Acts records, is in full surge. It is class-blind and color-blind and age-blind, and it comes to the simple person as well as to the genius. Given a yielding, it will pour through the lives of ordinary lay men and women and through its power will release them for hallowed service in the fabric of this world.

Douglas Steere, 1969

. . . The Spirit which led me forth,
was to me like a needle of a compass,
touched with a loadstone;
for so it pointed where I ought to go,
and when I came to the far end of the journey.

Esther Palmer, 1704

A spiritual leading from God will:

~ Lead to expressing love and light. . . .
~ Be confirmed by others. . . .
~ Come with clarity, initially or gradually. . . .
~ Lead into service to others. . . .
~ Resonate with one's deepest desires. . . .
~ Require periods of rest. . . .
~ Not be ego-driven. . . .
~ Be persistent. . . .
~ Be in harmony with the essence of the life and teachings of Jesus. . . .
~ Lead to more love, joy, peace, and patience. . . .

A person who has persisted in spiritual faithfulness for many years will often show signs of the biblical fruits of the Spirit, "love, joy, peace, patience, kindness, goodness, faithfulness, gentleness, and self-control." (Galatians 5:22–23)

Charlotte Lyman Fardelmann, 2001

I would hesitate to claim that I receive direct guidance from God—I do not hear a divine voice that tells me what to do. But I do have a sense that I am being drawn to take one course of action rather than another. The guidance, however, arises from a countless number of experiences, influences, attitudes, and disciplines, which I have accumulated over the years and upon which I have reflected.

George H. Gorman, 1973

God doesn't usually tell us what to do in so many words. But it's amazing how the world offers nudges once we ask! Suddenly, books open to significant passages. Being with our child brings an awareness. Chance events reveal opportunities to give our gifts or satisfy our needs. Messages may come during dreams, meditation, or prayer, in the form of images, words, or feelings in our bodies. Or we may wake up one morning with that feeling of knowing. We find God by paying attention to the present moment.

Julie Shaul, 1999

One summer day during his lunch hour, William Ditzler (1821–1897) was suddenly led to take his Bible and read aloud standing beside an open window in his office. Day after day for several weeks, he stood beside the open window and read. Then, a voice seemed to say, "It is enough."

Some time later, a clergyman from a neighboring church came to see William. "I feel I should tell you of an experience of one of my parishioners," he explained. "Is she anyone I know?" William asked. "I think not. She was a young girl who lived in an upper room across the courtyard from your office. Although she knew she was dying of tuberculosis, she had become bitter toward God and refused to meet with me. Then one day, the voice of an unseen, unknown reader came to her. She tried not to listen. She put her hands over her ears and pulled up the covers. Still the voice came day after day. Gradually she began to listen and she died in great peace."

Based on information from Marie Haines, 1972

Follow your conscience, if you feel certain,
but do not refuse to open any window of your soul to new light.

The General Conference of Friends in India, 1969

Pray the Eternal to grease your weathercock
so that it turn well at the true wind of the Spirit
and not remain caught by the rust of tradition
in a position unrelated to truth.

Pierre Ceresole, A prayer written in India during the 1930s

. . . I have always been heartened by the reluctance of Moses in responding to God's call. Here was no valiant dashing into action, fearless unquestioning confrontation with the power-base of Pharaoh. In fact, according to the rather honest story in Exodus, he makes every excuse in the book. He asks how he is to describe God to Pharaoh; then what to do if the people won't believe him; then rather touchingly, "I have never been eloquent; I am slow of tongue and slow of speech"; finally the most honest answer of all, "O my Lord, please send someone else!" I think we've all been there with Moses at some point in our lives.

Helen Steven, 2005

One of the little tricks I have for avoiding a leading is to tell God that I will take it under advisement. "Good idea, God. Let me think it over and I will get back to you. In about thirty years." But the trick doesn't work. Not really. Because if it's a true leading you know you are turning it down.

Bill Kreidler, 1994

If we ignore an insight,
we are less able to perceive the next one.
If we are not open to leadings,
we will be less able to know them when they come.

Paul A. Lacey, 1985

Dear Hearts,
you make your own troubles,
by being unwilling and disobedient to that which would lead you.
I see there is no way but to go hand in hand with God in all things,
running after God without fear or considering,
leaving the whole work only to God.
If God seem to smile, follow in fear and love;
and if God seem to frown,
follow, and fall into God's will,
and you shall see God is yours still.

James Nayler, 1653

We have all looked at the deeds of others and said, "I could never do that." That is not the point. Heroism is not necessarily about great dramatic deeds of daring. We are not called to imitate each other's actions, nor to feel disempowered by our failure to be what we are not. We are called to be faithful, to follow our own inner leadings, in our own time, using the particular and special gifts that are unique to each one of us. . . .

Helen Steven, 2005

I think I have wasted a great deal of my life waiting to be called to some great mission which would change the world. I have looked for important social movements. I have wanted to make a big and important contribution to the causes I believe in. I think I have been too ready to reject the genuine leadings I have been given as being matters of little consequence. It has taken me a long time to learn that obedience means doing what we are called to do even if it seems pointless or unimportant or even silly. . . . We need to develop our own unique social witness, in obedience to God. We need to listen to the gentle whispers, which will tell us how we can bring our lives into greater harmony with heaven.

Deborah Haines, 1978

Spiritual discernment is a process of going deeper. It is drawing on one's whole self, heart, mind, soul, and spirit. It includes and transcends intellectual analysis. It includes and transcends emotional intelligence. It is the bringing together of all of one's faculties within the larger context of the transcendent. . . . Spiritual discernment is practiced both individually and corporately. Even when done individually, it is never in isolation. Individual and corporate discernment dance together, hand in hand. Corporate discernment requires prepared hearts and minds of the individuals involved. Individual discernment requires the support of a community, nurturing and grounding the person's spiritual life. Individual discernment also requires the accountability of a community, offering checks and balances to the individual's discernment.

Margaret Benefiel, 2005

The way I tend to do on-going life discernment
is by keeping an open ear cocked inside
as I think about what I'm going to do today,
as I think about the focus of the next week, next month, or next year.
As [my husband] and I talk about things,
I do it with the feeling that I am listening
with an inner ear as to what feels right,
what sits well, what feels comfortable.

Fran Tabor, 2001

God seems not to shout at us very much—it is just not God's style. As the prophet learned, God is not in the earthquake or the tornado, but in the still, small voice that persists in the silence afterward. So while it is always useful to pray that God will speak up, it is good policy to be enfolding ourselves in silence at the same time. This is the via negativa. I may not be able to tell which voice is God's in my life today, but I can pick out one that is not God, and silence it or eliminate it from my life. Then I can pick out another one that is not God, and quiet that voice as well. If I keep on with this process, God's voice will come to stand out more and more, as there is less and less competition for my attention and loyalty.

Lloyd Lee Wilson, 1998

Early Friends used the tests of
moral purity,
patient waiting,
self-consistency of the spirit,
and group unity
as criteria in their discernment process.

Hugh Barbour, 1964

Martha Penzer experienced a feeling of "aha!" when she read a bulletin board announcement for a peace pilgrimage commemorating the fiftieth anniversary of the end of World War II. The pilgrimage was to begin with a fast and vigil at Auschwitz-Birkenau, and then prayerfully process through many of the world's troubled places before ending at Hiroshima, Japan. Martha's father had been imprisoned in Auschwitz-Birkenau during World War II, and the strong Aha! she felt on reading the announcement for the pilgrimage took her by surprise, because she knew she needed to be part of the pilgrimage. There had been numerous opportunities in the past for Martha to return to Poland, but she had never before felt led to go.

Friends are interdependent mystics who rely on one another for help in discerning their leadings and for support in following them.[13] So in the manner of Friends, Martha wrote to her Meeting asking for help to discern (prayerfully consider) the truth about this "tickling that wouldn't leave her alone." The Meeting appointed a clearness committee who prayed with her about joining the peace pilgrimage and asked her hard, clarifying questions. Satisfied with the spiritual integrity of her response, Martha's clearness committee then reported back to the meeting that Martha was following an authentic leading. So the Meeting then appointed a support committee whose members assisted her by raising funds, helped her test her physical stamina by walking with her a full day, and went with her to buy warm clothes. Once Martha started the pilgrimage her support committee kept in touch, and prayed for her throughout the months-long walk.

*Based on information from Charlotte Lyman Fardelmann
and Martha Penzer, 2001*

The Spirit wants . . . our peacemaking efforts to succeed.
If we are willing to follow our leadings—
to be followers of God rather than trying to lead God—
we will be brought to what we need to do
and given what we need to do it.

Mary Lord, 1996

Queries

When have I had a sense of being nudged or led by God? What happened when I did or did not follow the leading?

Before following a leading, am I willing to prayerfully probe my motives and acknowledge my self-will? Am I willing to engage others in helping me be clear about my leading?

When discerning my personal leadings, or helping others discern theirs, do I use the traditional tests of "moral purity, patient waiting, self-consistency of the spirit, and group unity" as criteria in my discernment process? [14]

Practicing Peace with Ourselves through Faith

Let not loyalty and faithfulness forsake you;
bind them about your neck,
write them on the tablet of your heart.

Proverbs 3:3

In 1680, King Charles II of England gave William Penn a large tract of land in the New World in repayment for a debt, and the king dubbed the land Pennsylvania (meaning Penn's woods). William used this land to create a "holy experiment" based on his faith that it is possible to build the Commonwealth of God on earth.[15]

William began by compensating the Native Americans living in Pennsylvania for their land, which helped create an atmosphere of trust between the Native Americans and the homesteaders. While many settlers in the colonies surrounding Pennsylvania lived in constant fear of armed conflicts with Native Americans, the Quaker colonists in Pennsylvania walked about unarmed, visiting native families in their wigwams and inviting them into their homes. Some Quakers left their children with native neighbors when attending religious gatherings in Philadelphia, and there are stories of Native Americans returning children lost in the woods.[16]

Nineteenth-century academic Isaac Sharpless wrote about Pennsylvania "that for seventy years there was neither war nor rebellion, the frontiers were secure without forts, and the harbors without men-of-war."[17] As a further reflection of his inclusive faith, William made Pennsylvania a place of religious toleration where dissenters could practice their religion freely, so it was not plagued by the witch hunts and religious strife of some other colonies. William's children and others, however, later fell away from his faith, and William's original vision of his "holy experiment" held only as long as Friends governed the colony. But despite this fact, what happened in Pennsylvania continues to serve as a historical model of governance based on a faithful adherence to justice, tolerance, and peace.[18]

William's efforts affected history in ways he could not have imagined. His Frame of Government for Pennsylvania was used by American colonists as a reference for writing the U.S. Constitution, and his "holy experiment" in Pennsylvania continues to inspire peaceable communities around the globe.[19]

William Penn did not set out to change the world; he simply tried to faithfully build God's Commonwealth on Earth. By allowing his faith to guide him, however, the world was transformed by his example of faithful living, his vision of just government, and his practice of peacemaking.

To Friends everywhere,
we do not ask that you pray that we be safe.
We ask that you pray that we be faithful.

France Yearly Meeting, 1943, written during a time of war and Nazi occupation

True faith is not assurance, but the readiness to go forward experimentally, without assurance. It is a sensitivity to things not yet known. . . . For what we apprehend of truth is limited and partial, and experience may set it all in a new light; if we too easily satisfy our urge for security by claiming that we have found certainty, we shall no longer be sensitive to new experiences of truth.

Charles Carter, 1971

In Sanskrit the word for faith is "sraddha" from "to set" and "heart." In this sense faith is an activity of setting the heart. Whether expressed in religious or secular terms, having faith may be understood as the activity of making meaning—composing and being composed by what we trust as ultimately true and dependable. Thus, faith is not just something that religious people have. Faith—meaning-making in its most comprehensive dimensions—is something that all human beings do in the everyday dialogue between fear and trust, hope and hopelessness, power and powerlessness, alienation and belonging.

Laurent A. Parks Daloz, Cheryl H. and James P. Keen,
and Sharon Daloz Parks, 1996

Faith it has been said,
Is not trying to believe something regardless of the evidence.
Faith is trying to do something regardless of the consequences.

Kathleen Lonsdale, 1954

. . . If we would stand against the hurricane, we need roots that run deep. I know that for all of us, on those rare occasions when we have found the courage, the will, to put principle above convenience, there is a deep and profound gratitude for a faith that goes beyond knowing.

Stephen G. Cary, 2003

Dare we,
trusting in heaven,
take the risks required of us if we would live out our truth within?
There's no such thing as a risk without fear,
and acting on new insights is daring.
Dare we let go of our precious security?
Dare we abandon seeking the fruits of our efforts?
Dare we relinquish our comfort zones—
knowing the risks may bring us disaster?

Gene Knudsen Hoffman, 1997

Our human desire for simple answers extends into our understanding of God and faith. We want to know what is real and true. We don't especially like ambiguity or complexity, even in our religious beliefs. Our rational minds struggle with paradoxes, when two seemingly conflicting realities are both true. We want there to be one right answer. . . .

God's ways are better than ours, but up close they can seem mighty peculiar and even unnerving. Part of what we are called to do as we work toward establishing God's realm here on Earth is to give up our human desire to understand and be in control of everything. If we can learn to live with paradox, then we can learn to trust God more fully. If, on the other hand, we still need to lean on the crutch of easy answers, then our faith is not yet as strong as it could be.

Cathy Habschmidt, 2004

If we lived with blazing certainties and well lit paths through the wilderness we would not need faith at all. It is about living with "uncertainties, mysteries, and doubts" and with what the mystical tradition calls the via negativa. Although we may prefer bright and breezy affirmations of faith, there are actually vast tracts of unknowing and inner darkness to be negotiated, and like Dostoevsky, our hallelujahs must often come out of "the crucible of doubt."

Jo Farrow, 1990

The experience of God may be rare or frequent,
but few of us experience God at all times.
During the intervals we need faith.
Faith requires us to act as though
we were aware of God's presence at all times.

Anne Curo, 2003

We have heard it said again and again that Christianity has not so much failed as that it has not yet been tried. . . . Those who have shared in the experiment have no illusions about the difficulties or the blemishes. They are extremely humble over the role they have played and the thing they have accomplished. Their one concern has been, and is, to keep the faith and to follow the gleam.

Rufus M. Jones, 1923

I said to one of the Cuban Friends, "It must be hard to be a Christian in Cuba." He smiled. "Not as hard as it is in the United States," he said. Of course, I asked why he said that, and he went on, "You are tempted by three idols that do not tempt us. One is affluence, which we do not have. Another is power, which we also do not have. The third is technology, which again we do not have. Furthermore, when you join a church or a meeting, you gain social acceptance and respectability. When we join, we lose those things, so we must be very clear about what we believe and what the commitment is that we are prepared to make."

Gordon M. Browne, Jr., 1989

. . . God appears in the midst of crisis to bring us peace,
but we must walk on the waters with faith,
and when it seems that the waves will drown us,
there will always be a hand—God's hand,
to pull us out from what may feel like the bottom of the sea.

Ramon Gonzalez Longoria Escalon, 2005

I know not what the future has
Of marvel or surprise,
Assured alone that life and death
God's mercy underlies
And if my heart and flesh are weak
To bear an untried pain,

The bruised reed God will not break,
But strengthen and sustain.

John Greenleaf Whittier, 1867

Is it fair to say that the Christian world *believes* in Christ's teaching? Hear his words. . . . "Thou shalt love the Lord thy God with all thy heart, and with all thy soul, and with all thy mind. This is the first and great commandment. And the second is like unto it. Thou shalt love thy neighbor as thyself." . . . If people *believed* this teaching of Christ, could there be any provocation or any resort to war? If people *believed* that it is a great commandment, "Thou shalt love thy neighbor as thyself," would the century just closing have recorded with all its attendant horrors the slaughter in battle of 4,470,000 men? Alas! This is our terrible unbelief. "Lord help our unbelief!"

Elizabeth Powell Bond, 1895

. . . I want there should be a fullness of faith
in the possibility of removing mountains on the side of right.
If we believe that war is wrong,
and everyone must,
then we ought to believe
that by proper efforts on our part
it may be done away with.

Lucretia Mott, Mother's Peace Festival, June 2, 1876

In faith we go forward,
With breathtaking boldness,
And in faith we stand still,
Unshaken, with amazing confidence.

Thomas R. Kelly, 1941

Queries

Do I live as if I were aware of God's presence at all times? How is my faith reflected in my daily life?

What has restored my faith after my faith has been shattered?

How does my practice of peace reflect my faith? When has my faith given me the courage to take risks in practicing peace?

Chapter 2

Practicing Peace in our Everyday Lives with

Love

Parenting and Mentoring

Community

Money and Resources

Plain Living and Simplicity

The Earth

Beauty, Joy, and Gratitude

Practicing Peace in our Everyday Lives with Love

If I speak in the tongues of people and of angels,
but have not love, I am a noisy gong or a
clanging cymbal. And if I have prophetic pow-
ers and understand all mysteries and all
knowledge, and if I have all faith, so as to
remove mountains, but have not love, I am
nothing.

1 Corinthians 13:1–2

John Woolman, an unassuming eighteenth-century tailor from New Jersey, spent over two decades paying prayerful visits to Friends still holding slaves, and he wrote in his journal that these visits had "no cause to promote but the cause of pure universal love."[1] Many abolitionists debated, argued, and ranted against slavery, but John simply held unconditional love in his heart for both the slave owners and the slaves. Since "love was the first motion" for his visits, he was careful not to shame either the slaves or the slaveholders.[2]

One expression of this love was that he chose to wear only linen clothes because cotton was grown by slaves. And when he ate food prepared by slaves, or benefited from slave labor in any way, he gave his hosts money for the services he received and encouraged them to give this money to their slaves directly as wages. Love is difficult to resist and has a way of searching our souls and enlarging our hearts. So when the slave owners felt Divine Love radiating through John's gentle words and personal integrity, their hearts were opened, and the seeds of his anti-slavery message fell into spiritually prepared ground.

By 1783, American Quakers, inspired in large part by John Woolman's ministry of unconditional love, had released their slaves, and the Religious Society of Friends became the first religious community in the United States to both free their slaves and advocate for emancipation.[3] Still today God is calling to each of us, encouraging us to practice peace by taking up the holy work of saving the world through love.

It seems no doubt a bit of religious aristocratic pride in the midst of the welter of bombed cities and invaded countries and war camps and actual slums and sinking ships and unfed children to talk of the progress of the soul and the immortal beauty of love. . . . Our danger, however, is not that we shall talk of love in too exalted terms, but that we shall treat it in too commonplace a fashion. If love is to be the spring and source of the progress of the soul, as Plato and Dante and Emerson . . . have prophesied, it must have a touch of eternity to it, and it must bring an unwonted splendor to life.

Rufus M. Jones, 1944

Love is God's name,
Love is God's Nature,
Love is God's life.

Sarah Blackborow, 1658

When our eyes are opened
to see that the Power of the universe
is steadily focused toward us in love,
we can scarcely do anything else
but tremble.

Howard R. Macy, 1988

I'd like to think God loves me because of my sterling character and pleasant demeanor, but when I suggest this possibility, my wife's uncontrollable laughter quickly deflates such delusions. It seems much more likely that God loves every person as much as God loves me. I believe God is love and that everything God does, God does because of love. When this love is poured on the wicked, the rebellious, and the resistant—adjectives that fit all of us on occasion—we call it grace.

Phillip Gulley and James Mulholland, 2004

In learning to love ourselves and others
we are always in the shallows
of what is, after all,
a vast and unfathomable ocean.
We may splash in the shallows,
wade in further
and even swim out bravely until we are out of our depth
but we shall never manage to navigate more
than a small expanse of it.

Jo Farrow, 1990

One gives up all one has for . . . the love that resides in the self, the self-love, out of which all love pours. The fountain, the source. At the center. One gives up all the treasured sorrow and self-mistrust, all the precious loathing and suspicion, all the secret triumphs of withdrawal. One bends in the wind. There are many disciplines that strengthen one's athleticism for love. It takes all one's strength. And yet it takes all one's weakness too. Sometimes it is only by having all one's so-called strength pulverized that one is weak enough, strong enough, to yield. It takes that power of nature in one which is neither strength nor weakness but closer perhaps to virtue, personalized energy. . . . Bear ye one another's burdens, God said, and God was talking law. Love is not a doctrine, Peace is not an international agreement. Love and Peace are beings who live as possibilities in us.

Mary Caroline Richards, 1962

Slowly we learn that we are all broken,
all less than perfect,
and that God loves us,
each one,
wonderfully even so.
Slowly we learn that the real love for one another we crave
is not the ideal love of my personal facade for your facade,
but the imperfect intent to love that my flawed self can offer to
  the real you.

Lloyd Lee Wilson, 2001

What love is free from pain?
A painless love is beyond our imagination.
A mother holding an infant in her arms feels a pang,
as though a sword had pierced her breast.
A lover looking in the face of his beloved thinks of the pain of
  parting.
A child basking in its mother's love
is suddenly warned of the time when she will be taken away from it.
Show me a love that is devoid of sorrow and pain,
and I will show you a false and shallow love.

Inazo Nitobe, 1938

The problem comes when we meet the unlovable;
how is that to be loved?
. . . Whether or not a person was "unlovable" was beside the point,
they were made to be loved,
and only being loved makes a person lovable.

Harold Loukes, 1960

[Jack Kornfeld] said, more or less,
"At the end of your life the only question worth asking is,
"Did I love enough?"
My internal answer was,
"Of course I haven't, and perhaps never will."

But I can begin trying.
Whatever happens, it will keep me well occupied for the rest of
    my life. . . ."
Life is full of not-knowing-how-to-love
and finding new ways to act,
to be, to respond, to live.
Since I think this may take several lifetimes,
I can't waste any more time.

Gene Knudsen Hoffman, 2003

But though hate rises in enfolding flame
At each renewed oppression, soon it dies:
It sinks as quickly as we saw it rise,
While love's small constant light burns still the same.
Know this: though love is weak and hate is strong,
Yet hate is short, and love is very long.

Kenneth E. Boulding, 1945

God triumphs over evil and pain and death,
Not by combating them with the weapons of this world,
But by continuing to love.

Susan Furry, 1981

Where is the love going to come from
to transform human violence into peaceful societies,
if not from a more developed human spirituality?

Elise Boulding, 1996

I was overseeing Quaker relief programs in Europe after the
Second World War. I had called a meeting in Amsterdam of representatives from our relief units scattered across the continent. . . .
There was low morale in the scattered units, isolated and lonely .
and stressed, struggling imperfectly to succor the needy . . . we
were a discouraged company. Our contribution was so small and

imperfect and the need so great. Suddenly a Dutch Friend burst in, holding aloft a newspaper with a banner headline: "Quakers win Nobel Peace Prize . . . honored for relief service. . . ." Stunned silence . . . silence that quickly became a Quaker meeting for worship. . . . There was only a single message, from a young worker in devastated Poland: "All I can say is—a little love goes a long way."

Stephen G. Cary, 2003

Queries

When has my life been transformed by love? When has my love helped transform the lives of others?

When have I been wounded by love? How has my life been different as a result of that experience?

What sacrifices has love demanded of me?

What trials in my current life might be able to be turned around by seeing them as challenges to love? [4]

Have I loved enough? Whom might God be calling me to love more?

Practicing Peace in our Everyday Lives
with Parenting and Mentoring

Only take heed, and keep your soul diligently,
lest you forget the things which your eyes have seen,
and lest they depart from your heart
all the days of your life;
make them known to your children
and your children's children.

Deuteronomy 4:9

During the 1850s in Philadelphia, a young Quaker girl, Hannah Severn, longed to wear colorful dresses and hoop skirts like her peers. She especially resented having to wear a plain, unfashionable bonnet, which identified her as having values embarrassingly different from those of her more worldly friends. Her parents tried hard to model their faith by living with simplicity, equality, integrity, and peace, but Hannah resented the ways these values set her apart. She did keep wearing her plain clothes, but the story is told that she sometimes rebelled by borrowing colorful sashes and by throwing her detested bonnet down the stairs.[5]

One afternoon while running an errand for her mother, Hannah heard someone whisper to her from the dark recesses of a small side alley. When she ventured into the shadows, she discovered a runaway slave woman and her baby who had been without adequate food or shelter for days. That night Hannah and her parents rescued the woman and her infant, harboring them in their home where they eventually nursed them back to health and helped them make their next connection north on the Underground Railroad. But before departing, the slave woman told Hannah about waiting two days for someone in a plain bonnet to walk by because she had heard that Quakers wore plain clothes and could be trusted to help. From that time on, Hannah Severn did not resent her simple clothes and bonnet because she now understood and respected the trustworthiness and compassionate values they represented.[6]

Rufus M. Jones wrote that "Something of God comes into our world with every child that is born. There is here with the newborn child a divine spark, a light within. . . ."[7] And since we can see in each child's eyes an inimitable reflection of that divine spark, our work as parents and mentors is not to make our children in our image, but to share with them the religious beliefs and moral values that we find life-giving. Parenting and mentoring involve walking a fine line between honoring our children's uniqueness by listening and learning from them, and guiding them, as best we can, by the example of our lives toward that which we believe to be good, wise, and holy.

It has never been easy to pass wisdom and spiritual values from one generation to the next. Today's prevalence of individualism, materialism, and violence, however, make imparting wisdom, spirituality, and peace to young people an even more difficult, but especially crucial, task, requiring of parents and mentors patience, empathy, faith, uncommon sense, and unconditional love.

Our children are given to us for a time to cherish, to protect, to nurture, and then to salute as they go their separate ways. They too have the light of God within, and a family should be a learning community in which children not only learn skills and values from parents, but, in which adults learn new ways of experiencing things and seeing things through young eyes. From their birth on, let us cultivate the habit of dialogue and receptive listening. We should respect their right to grow into their own wholeness, not just the wholeness we may wish for them.

Elizabeth Watson, 1980

As a futurist I have long been convinced
that families are the primary agents of social change in any society.
It is in this setting that individuals first become aware
that the passage of time means growth and change,
that tomorrow is never like yesterday.
It is in this setting that one's first daydreams
about a different future take place.
I have come to find the phrase "the Tao of family" meaningful
because it reflects the special nature of the family as directioned
    movement.
Tao means the Way
and the Tao of family is the Way of family into the future.

Elise Boulding, 1989

Where two or three are gathered, someone spills the milk. . . . A family that can live with each other's idiosyncrasies can discover joy, one of the main ingredients in communion with God and each other. Who is to say that a prayer for the renewed health of three sick guppies by an eight-year-old is not just as efficacious as one in the King James English quoted verbatim from the Book of Common Prayer? In fact, which is more common? . . .

Mealtime for many of us can be more sacramental than it is, possibly by practicing better habits of discipline but, more likely, by letting it be a time for sharing, listening, laughing, and enjoying each other. In fact, we may draw closer to God when milk can be spilled without anger and recrimination, when a child is free to pray what they feel and not by rote, and especially—would you believe—when your teenager *volunteers* to do the dishes.

O God, Help us not to cry over spilt milk. . . . Amen.

Tom Mullen, 1973

How many daily occasions there are for the exercise of patience, forbearance, benevolence, good humor, cheerfulness, candor, sincerity, compassion, self-denial! How many instances occur of satirical hints, of ill-natured witticisms, of fretfulness, impatience, strife, and envy; besides those of disrespect, discontent, sloth, and very many other seeds of evil. . . . When we consider that private life also has its trials, temptations, and troubles, it ought surely to make us vigilant, when around our own fire-side, lest we should quiet our apprehensions, and cease from our daily watchfulness.

John Barclay, 1814

Family life exposes all of our dirty little secrets: anger, impatience, nastiness, and desire to control others. One Friend said it well: vile. If we come clean, don't we all behave in vile ways at home sometimes, children and parents alike? Parenting revealed to me all the stubborn wounds stemming from my own childhood, re-opened with little provocation: feelings of insecurity, inadequacy, unworthiness. These are my "disabilities of the heart." Good news! God accepts us, dis-abilities and all. God recognizes our inner beauty and calls us to grow toward greater maturity. . . . When we acknowledge these not fully matured parts of ourselves and bring them into God's love, we can be guided in how to nurture these parts and resolve conflict more creatively. . . . When we live this way of the heart, and discover Christ dwelling in the smallness and weakness within ourselves and our children, our families can grow in freedom toward God.

Mary Kay Rehard, 2002

One autumn day about a year ago, I listened as a young mother in meeting rose to deliver a message that has stayed with me ever since: "Prepare for the best." Her words were simple and heart-felt. She told us that her very young daughter repeatedly had been asking to bring her favorite doll to meeting. This mother steadfastly refused to grant her request. Then it occurred to her to ask why her daughter wanted to bring the doll to meeting. With some emotion this young mother shared that her little daughter wanted her doll to experience meeting for worship. She realized that she'd been trying to avert something undesirable, when what her daughter wanted was something to be cherished.

Susan Corson-Finnerty, 2000

A family reared in the atmosphere of love, where each defers to the other, consulting each other's tastes and inclinations, where words of request and entreaty are used instead of command and a sense of peace and gentleness pervades the household, may be sure that those who go forth from its influence will do good in the world by a noble and peaceable example.

Home is the spring whence all the streams which make up the ocean of life are flowing. Let us strive then to make it the abode of cheerfulness, forbearance and love, that all people may, in time, learn to dwell together in peace, and find upon Earth a foretaste of the joy of eternal heaven.

Content Whipple, 1873

I was not "christened" in a church, but I was sprinkled from morning to night with the dew of religion. We never ate a meal together which did not begin with a hush of thanksgiving; we never began a day without "a family gathering" at which my mother read a chapter of the Bible, after which there would fol- low a weighty silence. . . . My first steps in religion were thus acted. It was a religion we did together. Almost nothing was said in the way of instructing me. We all joined together to listen for God and then one of us talked to God for the others. In these simple ways my religious disposition was being unconsciously formed and the roots of my faith in unseen realities were reaching down far below my crude and childish surface thinking.

Rufus M. Jones, 1926

God, make us worthy of the children we serve.

*Violet Zaru, administrator of the Quaker Play Center in Ramallah,
recorded by Beth Parrish, 2004*

The false love of glory, the cruel spirit of revenge,
the blood-thirsty ambition, swelling the breast of the soldier in
 the battlefield;
these are often the ripened harvest from the seed sown by their

parent's hands,
when in their childish hours they gave them tiny weapons,
and taught them to mimic war's murderous game.

Anonymous, but presumed to be written by Lucretia Mott, 1846

While there is a great deal written on providing love and security
for children so they won't grow into hostile adults, there is nothing very much on how you raise children to be sufficiently alienat-
ed from society so they won't accept things "as they are," and
sufficiently identified with it so that they will contribute in creative ways to the building of a better social order. . . . [W]e still
don't know much about producing children who will irrepressibly
dream about a better society than the one we have, and obstinate-
ly work for its realization.

Elise Boulding, 1961

Our children will inherit from us a world very different from the
world we would like to have left them. We would like to leave
them a safe world, a peaceful world, a comfortable world. It is
more like a smoldering volcano. Yet it is still a world of great
opportunities for adventure, it is still God's world, it is still a
world in which they may hear the voice of Jesus saying, even as he
sends them out to work for him: "Peace I leave with you, my
peace I give unto you: not as the world giveth, give I unto you.
Let not your heart be troubled, neither let it be afraid."

Kathleen Lonsdale, 1953

. . . I entreat you watch over the younger for good,
and be good patterns and Holy examples to them,
and use all diligence to admonish, and counsel,
with much tenderness in the wisdom and power of God.

Theophila Townsend, 1686

Queries

How am I respecting and nurturing the uniqueness of each child in my life?

How has what I have learned from children affected or changed my life?

Do I evaluate my activities with children by asking the question: "Will this help the children grow up to be peacemakers?" [8]

Do I convey a sense of hopefulness to the children in my life, and do I foster in them the imagination and confidence that they can make a difference in the world?

Practicing Peace in our Everyday Lives
with Community

"For where two or three
are gathered in my name,
There am I in the midst of them."

Matthew 18:20

In 2002, Frances Crowe, a dedicated social activist in her mid-eighties, was part of a small community peace group from Northampton, Massachusetts, that tried unsuccessfully for months to schedule an appointment with their congressman concerning the impending war with Iraq. The congressman, who supported the idea of going to war, was reluctant to have his position challenged, so he steadfastly refused to meet with Frances's group.

Finally, Frances and her frustrated colleagues decided that perhaps the congressman would listen to a larger community delegation. So they invited others from the community whom the congressman would recognize to join them in serenading him at his home. Among those asked were local ministers, teachers from the congressman's children's school, and other well-known community leaders.

Early one Sunday evening, the large, neatly dressed community delegation arrived at the congressman's house and began a serenade of beautiful peace songs, complete with harmonies. After about a half hour of melodious singing, the congressman came out of his house smiling. He invited the group to sit on the lawn while he listened carefully for ninety minutes to their concerns about initiating a war with Iraq. When they left he thanked them warmly for coming.

The next day a newspaper reporter called Frances Crowe and said, "I understand that you were part of the community group that serenaded Congressman Neal with peace songs last evening." The reporter went on to say that the congressman told him the peaceful message from the community had helped change his mind, and he was now prepared to vote against the war.[9]

We need one another to build God's peaceful commonwealth. When we gather in community, each of us brings his or her piece of God's harmonious truth, so our voices resonate deeper, louder, and clearer, thus strengthening and amplifying our individual calls for peace on earth.

[Jesus said] "For where two or three are gathered in my name,
I am there among them." . . .
Gandhi would have been just another Hindu holy man
without the tens of thousands who gathered to march to the sea
    to make salt
and who committed their lives to nonviolence.
Martin Luther King, Jr., would have been just another minister
without the people who gathered to march and fill the jails.
God is too big to be fully manifested in one person.
God requires an entire people.

Will Taber, 2003

The peaceable commonwealth is by definition a vision of community.
It is a vision of renewed relationships:
between people and God,
among people,
and between people and the rest of God's creation.

Sandra Cronk, 1984

This is how God intended it to be among the human beings and God's self . . . a triangle made up of God, my neighbor, and myself. In Burundian villages many people make a fire between three stones and place a clay pot on them for cooking their food.

I have never heard of anyone being able to cook on only two stones. In fact it is dangerous, because if you manage to warm the water on the two stones, by the time the water boils, the pot will get agitated, fall down and burn whoever is near. A faith that only exists between you and your God, like a pot on only two stones, is an incomplete faith.

David Niyonzima and Lon Fendall, 2001

I was in California a few years ago, and I had never been to California before. I'm from Iowa and I'd never seen the redwood trees other than in picture books. I was amazed at their height, feeling thankful for the redwood trees, and thinking how deep their roots must go to hold up a tree so tall. And in meeting for worship that very day, a Friend rose and said something like, "You know these redwood trees? You'd think their roots go really deep, but their roots go out really wide. They spread out to each other and entangle with each other, and give each other support and that's how they stand and grow so tall, and that's how they weather the storms."

That's what community is about! We do want our own spiritual roots to go deep, but as they grow deep, they can also be growing out and intertwining with others, supporting each other against the wind and the rain and the storms in the Spirit.

And, as the tree grows up, the roots are still growing out. It's not one or the other. They grow in both directions at the same time.

Deborah Fisch, 2003

The first fulfillment of Jesus' promise [at Pentecost] came in
    community
so everyone could see the Spirit as a single source
as its flames rested on everyone.
In this setting, it would be impossible for a few people
to claim the Spirit came to them, but not to others.
It would also be impossible for someone to say,
"Well, I see there is a flame on everyone else's head,
but I'm sure there's no flame on my head.

I'm not worthy enough."
Since they couldn't see the flame on their own heads,
the community affirms what it sees,
"Yes, there is a flame on your head, too.
We are all one in the Spirit."

Janet Hoffman, 2002

The "lone Quaker" is an oxymoron. We are a Religious Society, a gathered people, who in community help each other listen, learn, and follow divine guidance. Our meetings provide encouragement and support. They supply warnings and admonitions when we need them. And, because we are all human, our meetings also provide the laboratory in which we inevitably hurt each other and can also heal, forgive, and learn to live together within God's enfolding love.

Martha Paxson Grundy, 2001

Human beings are such that life together always involves them in hurting one another in some way. People may want to disbelieve this, but even a brief exposure to real vulnerability will testify that it is so. In a desperate scramble to avoid this fact of life, people will remain distant and superficial with everyone. They will run to other churches or groups at the first sign of differences. They will clam up in a tight little shell that does not know how to cry . . . or laugh. Such a flight from reality is not life, but death. . . . If we want life, we must be prepared to hurt and be hurt. We simply must make peace with this fact. Once we accept this as a true perception of "life together," we can exert our energies learning how to deal with it, rather than attempting to avoid it.

Richard J. Foster, 1987

Safety in a community gets defined by how the most marginal person in the community is treated. We all believe that if people could see into our hearts and know who we really are, we too might be rejected, so we notice how those at the margins are welcomed.

Emily Sander, 1992

In true community we will not choose our companions,
For our choices are so often limited by self-serving motives. . . .
Instead our companions will be given to us by grace.
Often they will be persons who will upset our settled view of self
    and the world.
In fact, we might define true community as that place
Where the person you least want to live with lives. . . .

Parker J. Palmer, 1977

We have to learn to love difficult unlovable people. . . .
Part of the cost of discipleship
is living with the other disciples.

Beth Allen, 1984

You are commanded to love your neighbor,
not to ask your neighbor
to love you.

Damaris Parker-Rhodes, 1977

God comes to us in the midst of human need, and the most
pressing needs of our time demand community in response. How
can I participate in a fairer distribution of resources unless I live in
a community, which makes it possible to consume less? How can I
learn accountability unless I live in a community where my acts
and their consequences are visible to all? How can I learn to share
power unless I live in a community where hierarchy is unnatural?
How can I take the risks which right action demands, unless I
belong to a community which gives support? How can I learn the
sanctity of each life unless I live in a community where we can be
persons not roles to one another?

Parker J. Palmer, 1977

Friends, have you ever been flat out on your back, sick and
uncertain, paralyzed in fear, resigned in your depression? And

who carried you then? Who picked you up in love and faith and ushered you into a whole new order of being, who took you to the feet of the healer and held your hand when grace swept over you? Who in your life has done this holy work, pushing past your passivity, past your grief, and your woundedness?

And what about you? Do you not have strong arms? Who have you carried in the act of faithing? Who in your life have you loved past their feelings of hopelessness?

Are we not all gathered here today because there are those who carried us in faith to this moment in time, to this manifestation of the beloved community? And in our still, quiet moments in prayer, in worship, do we not hear a call to pick up and carry others, to be radiant in our faith—to be agents for life?

Beckey Phipps, 2004

We have a long, long way to go. So let us hasten along the road, the roads of human tenderness and generosity. Groping, we may find one another's hands in the dark.

Emily Green Balch, 1955

Queries

How is my faith community embodying and revealing God's presence in the world?

When there is conflict in my neighborhood, faith, or national community, do I hold the community in prayer and look for the good in each person's motivations?

When has my community helped carry me through a difficult time? Whom am I now helping to carry?

Practicing Peace in our Everyday Lives with Money and Resources

And all who believed were together
and had all things in common;
and they sold their possessions and goods
and distributed them all, as any had need.

Acts 2:45

In the summer of 1778, a British battleship intent on plunder sailed into Nantucket harbor and aimed its guns at the largely Quaker community. Despite the ship's blatant show of hostility, William Rotch, a well-respected Quaker elder, greeted the British commander, Sir Conway-Etherege, at the dock, and invited him home for dinner. After the meal, the commander, increasingly uncomfortable with his host's warm hospitality, announced that it was time for the plunder to begin.

The commander was shocked when William said that he should begin with his house because, as a successful businessman, he could absorb the loss better than some of his less prosperous neighbors. Not understanding why William would make such an unselfish and generous offer, the commander asked if there were other people like him in the community. William Rotch then took him to meet a merchant who had given four hundred barrels of flour to the poor during the previous winter and a shopkeeper who had given away blankets and shoes. Legend has it that the commander said that he could hardly believe that there were three such people in the whole world. He then returned to the battleship and, to the disappointment of his crew, sailed away.[10]

God calls us to share our resources with those in need. When we do not, economic disparities arise, causing disputes, social tensions, violence, and war. That is why right sharing of resources is a central issue in practicing peace.

Our attitude toward sharing our money and our material resources is essentially a spiritual matter. The Russian mystic and political philosopher Nicholas Berdyaev wrote, "Bread for myself is a material question, but bread for my neighbor is a spiritual question."[11] Our level of attention to the equitable sharing of our common wealth, especially to our treatment of the poor, is an indication of the spiritual health and ethic of any person, religious community, state, or nation.

A key vision for God's commonwealth is the biblical Jubilee—where everybody has enough and nobody has too much; where debts are forgiven and people are restored to their ancestral lands. Jubilee was a periodic redistribution of wealth, to prevent some people from staying wealthy at the expense of others.

When we accumulate an unfair portion of the world's wealth while so many others are poor, ill, hungry, and without resources or opportunity to improve themselves, we deny the vision of Jubilee and refuse to live into the Commonwealth of God, which is now coming into being on earth.

Lloyd Lee Wilson, 2003

For people of biblical faith, ancient covenants have grounded and guided economic practice. In the Book of Exodus, for example, we learn that when the Children of Israel were in the wilderness, God provided manna sufficient for each day, but if it was hoarded, it rotted. Later, if a neighbor borrowed your oxcart and left a coat in pledge, you had to be sure to give the coat back before sunset, even if the neighbor was not finished with the oxcart; this was especially binding if the neighbor was poor. A millstone could not be taken as a pledge because it was essential to a person's livelihood.

Sharon Daloz Parks, 1997

My generation grew up in the thirties, and the fear of poverty was burned into our souls. I lived for months on chili con carne at 10 cents a can. I lived in a slum because I had to. Like most of my contemporaries I hated and feared poverty. We did something about it—spent the next thirty years in exorcizing the devil of poverty by creating the affluent society. The magnitude of our success frightens us, but few of us have outgrown our fear of poverty. Only in my better moments of faith can I accept the saying of Jesus: "Therefore, take no thought, saying, What shall we eat? or What shall we drink? or Wherewithal shall we be clothed? For your God knoweth that ye have need of these things. But seek ye first the Commonwealth of God . . . and all these things shall be added unto you."

George Peck, 1973

. . . Rabbi Marcia Prager tells a story about a couple who had financial problems and argued about money. Prager ended up counseling the couple to adopt a traditional Jewish practice called tzedakah, which involves allocating a certain portion of one's income to helping the poor. "My assignment to them was to become givers—even if they could only give $2," she recalls. Prager says that assignment was a turning point for the couple; over time, they came to feel that they had enough, reduced their spending, and didn't fight so much about money. The secret? Prager thinks that giving changes our thinking: *we shift from thinking of ourselves as consumers to thinking of ourselves as guardians of the social welfare of our community.*

Prager's story illustrates an important point. Whether you give time, money, or both, focusing on helping other people with difficulties tends to put your problems in perspective. That can make you feel more fortunate and grateful.

Martha Mangelsdorf, 2003

. . . Just as nuclear warfare is only possible once a certain moral boundary concerning the treatment of others is breached, so an economic system based on wage-slavery and destitution depends on the acceptability of such death-in-life. . . . If grinding poverty of body, mind and spirit, and corresponding indifference to the health of the ecosystem, are not acceptable prices to pay for an economic system, then one has to find alternative systems. The law of maximal returns is not written in the stars but in our hearts and minds; it can be unwritten, as other laws have been before it.

Deborah Padfield, 1998

Everyone cheers when you give a cup of cold water to the suffering, but enthusiasm may wane when you ask why the cup was necessary, and what might be done to lessen the possibility that it might again be needed.

Stephen G. Cary, 2003

It is not enough to be generous, and give alms;
the enlarged soul, the true philanthropist,
is compelled by Christian principle
to look beyond the bestowing of a scant pittance
to the mere beggar of the day,
to the duty of considering the causes and sources of poverty.
We must consider how much we have done toward causing it.

Lucretia Mott, 1857

We've made charity—the bandaging of wounds—our focus and ignored how the sharp edges of our economic system tear and rip the poor. We give food to inner-city food pantries and fail to address the practice of the price gouging that plagues inner-city grocery stores. . . . We open soup kitchens and homeless shelters while applauding cuts in social programs and demanding lower taxes.

Phillip Gulley and James Mulholland, 2004

When you live in a nice community in a house where there is running water and electricity, attend good schools, have nice jobs and the crime rate is low, it is hard to understand that you have all of these comforts through the exploitation of other human beings. I can buy a portable CD player from Wal-mart for $30.00 because it was made in China where a person was paid $1.00 a week for working extraordinarily long hours. . . . We are a privileged country. Even our poor have so much more than the poor in other parts of the world.

Vanessa Julye, 2003

May we look upon our treasure,
the furniture of our houses, and our garments,
and try whether the seeds of war
have nourishment in these our possessions.

John Woolman, 1774

War is not an accident.
It is the logical outcome
of a certain way of life.

A.J. Muste, 1967

When visiting Honduras, I noticed every place of affluence—nice homes, the bank, Wendy's restaurant—had a guard with an M-16 standing outside. When I commented on this to a Honduran, he pointed out the United States does the same thing. We simply hide the weapons guarding our affluence in missile silos and nuclear submarines.

Phillip Gulley and James Mulholland, 2004

War takes place between nations.
And it also occurs inside our hearts
As our drive for more and more
pushes us further away from centeredness in God. . . .

Sandra Cronk, 1984

Queries

How do the financial and consumer choices I make in my daily life reflect my spiritual values?

How does sharing my resources (possessions, time, money) with those in need contribute to my sense of spiritual well-being and peace?

Where do I find seeds of war in my possessions and lifestyle?

How could our current economic system better support children, the poor, and those in need?

Practicing Peace in our Everyday Lives with Plain Living and Simplicity

Do not lay up for yourselves treasures on earth,
where moth and rust consume and where thieves
break in and steal, but lay up for yourselves
treasures in heaven, where neither moth nor
rust consumes and where thieves do not break in
and steal. For where your treasure is, there will
your heart be also.

Matthew 6:19–21

In 1986, Frank Levering, a young Hollywood screenwriter, and his wife Wanda Urbanska, a rising journalist, felt a growing hollowness at the center of their fast-paced lives. They decided their high-pressure lifestyle was keeping them from finding deeper, personal fulfillment, so they left California to seek a simpler lifestyle writing and tending the family cherry orchard in the Blue Ridge Mountains of Virginia. The hectic pace of life Frank and Wanda were fleeing is familiar to most of us. They wrote:

> We run on a treadmill, in many cases so time-starved that
> we'll cut someone off on the freeway if he threatens to swipe a
> few seconds from our precious reserve, or step on someone's
> sentence before she has a chance to complete it, or walk out of
> a meeting, a class, or even a church service if our attention
> starts to flag. There's always something else to do, some other,
> more pressing claim on our time. And so we rush through our
> minutes, our days—our lives—never quite taking hold of our-
> selves or the experience that we're supposed to be living.[12]

When Frank Levering and Wanda Urbanska stepped off the treadmill of busyness and material success that had given them one-dimensional lives, they had to make cultural and familial adjustments, and their hours in the orchard are sometimes long. But their quality of life and sense of spiritual fulfillment have steadily risen as they now have more time for their son, each other, hiking, gardening, writing, and watching the sunset from their front porch.[13]

We are living in frenetic and anxious times characterized by high material consumption and low personal fulfillment. Many of us are also experiencing an inner emptiness that we try to fill with busyness and shopping trips to the mall. The emptiness we feel, however, is most likely emanating from a place within described by philosopher Blaise Pascal as "an infinite abyss that can only be filled by an infinite and immutable object, that is to say, only by God."[14] Therefore, neither activities nor possessions will ever be able to satisfy the spiritual longing radiating from our souls. Plain living and simplicity, however, *can* remove the physical and emotional clutter from our lives, opening up more space for God, who alone has the power to bring deep peace and fulfillment into our lives.

Our lives in a modern city grow too complex and overcrowded. Even the necessary obligations which we feel we must meet grow overnight, like Jack's beanstalk, and before we know it we are bowed down with burdens, crushed under committees, strained, breathless, and hurried, panting through a never-ending program of appointments. . . . But if we withdraw from public engagements and interests, in order to spend quiet hours with the family, the guilty calls of citizenship whisper disquieting claims in our ears. Our children's schools should receive our interest, the civic problems of our community need our attention, the wider issues of the nation and the world are heavy upon us. Our professional status, our social obligations, our membership in this or that very important organization, put claims upon us. And in frantic fidelity we try to meet at least the necessary minimum of calls upon us. But we're weary, breathless. And we know and regret that our life is slipping away, with our having tasted so little of the peace and joy and serenity we are persuaded it should yield to a soul of wide caliber. The times for the deeps of the silences of the heart seem so few. And in guilty regret we must postpone till next week that deeper life of unshaken composure in the holy Presence, where we sincerely know our true home is, for this week is much too full.

Thomas R. Kelly, 1941

It is a witness to the spiritual poverty of our culture, for example, that in response to the question, "How are you?" we so often hear the answer, "I'm keeping busy," as if busyness were a guiding spiritual value or an adequate measure of our worth and achievement.

Howard R. Macy, 1988

A distinguished explorer, who spent a couple of years among the natives of the Upper Amazon . . . attempted a forced march through the jungle. The party made extraordinary speed for the first two days, but on the third morning, when it was time to start, the leader found all the natives sitting on their haunches, looking very solemn and making no preparations to leave. "They are waiting," the Chief explained to the explorer, "They cannot move farther until their souls have caught up with their bodies." Were these men acting on a truth we have forgotten? Is the world in chaos because it has neglected to wait for its soul?

A. Ruth Fry, 1950

It may surprise some of us to hear that the first generation of Friends did not have a testimony for simplicity. They came upon a faith, which cut to the root of the way they saw life, radically reorienting it. They saw that all they did must flow directly from what they experienced as true, and that if it did not, both the knowing and the doing became false. In order to keep the knowledge clear and the doing true, they stripped away anything which seemed to get in the way. They called those things superfluities, and it is this radical process of stripping for clear-seeing which we now term simplicity.

Frances Irene Taber, 1985

Outwardly, simplicity is shunning superfluities of dress, speech, behavior, and possessions, which tend to obscure our vision of reality. Inwardly, simplicity is spiritual detachment from the things of this world as part of the effort to fulfill the first commandment: to love God with all of the heart and mind and strength. . . . Simplicity does not mean drabness or narrowness but is essentially positive, being the capacity for selectivity in one who holds attention on the goal. Thus simplicity is an appreciation of all that is helpful towards living as children of the living God.

North Carolina Yearly Meeting of the Religious Society of Friends (Conservative), 1983

Do we buy a particular home on the basis of the call of God,
or because of the availability of money?
Do we buy a new car because we can afford it,
or because God instructed us to buy a new car?
If money determines what we do or do not do,
then money is our boss.
My money might say to me,
"You have enough to buy that,"
but my God might say to me,
"I don't want you to have it."
Now who am I to obey?

Richard J. Foster, 1989

When I was a newly convinced Friend, the executive secretary of Friends Meeting of Cambridge, Massachusetts, Elmer Brown, drove a large expensive-looking car—probably a Lincoln, though I don't remember for sure. What I remember is my disapproval that this weighty Friend should drive such an un-simple car! I was so upset that I finally cornered him in the parking lot and asked him how he could be so un-simple when our meeting looked to him to set an example for others. "Well," Elmer replied, "A Friend at the last meeting I served gave me this car so that I would have something to drive to carry out my responsibilities to the meeting. I didn't pay anything for it and it serves me well. That seems simple to me." Elmer was right and I was wrong: he was freed from a material worry to center his awareness on God, and I was distracted by the car away from attending to God.

Lloyd Lee Wilson, 1995

How easy it is to feel we are simple, peaceable, Spirit-led, faithful, when we may mostly be
conventionally moral, thrifty, and shy of conflict.
In the struggle to get past our comforting illusions,
and reach towards a God of truth,
whose love is also judgment,
and whose Light both convicts and heals us
to be stronger than we were before,
a habit of grappling with the Scriptures
at the levels of feelings, imagination, intellect,
and prayer is a powerful help indeed.

Brian Drayton, 2006

It would be consistent with a real awareness of human unity if I should invite into my house for a meal and a night's lodging a starving man who has knocked at my door. But if my rugs are so fine that I am afraid his dirty shoes may ruin them, I hesitate. If I have many valuable objects of art or much fine silverware, I also hesitate for fear he may pocket some of them or tell men who may later steal them from the house. If my furniture and hangings bespeak great wealth I mistrust him lest he hold me up; or perhaps if I am less suspicious and more courageous and more sensitively imaginative, I fear lest the contrast between his poverty and my abundance will make him secretly envious, or resentful, or bitter, or make him feel ill at ease. Or perhaps he is so very dirty that I fear he has vermin, and I am revolted by that thought and am so far from him humanly that I do not know how to deal with him humanely. In this case it is clear that my lack of simplicity acts as a barrier between him and me.

Richard B. Gregg, 1936

Men and women today try to achieve happiness by the pursuit of military and economic security, with the result that they find themselves in a world where, as Niebuhr has written recently of the USA, "the paradise of our domestic security is suspended in a hell of global insecurity"; or they equate happiness with the pursuit of pleasure, with the result that their leisure time is commercially exploited and they give themselves no time in which to think. They lose their simplicity and are easily affected by propaganda, particularly by the kind of propaganda that exploits selfishness and fear.

Kathleen Lonsdale, 1957

I expect I am not alone in my experience that part of what saps me (especially in the USA), part of what pulls me into some kind of unnamed despair, is the constant knowledge—often just beneath the surface—that I am daily participating in the pain of others. The knowledge that John Woolman would find . . . much "blood and suffering" in the clothes that I wear, the food that I eat, the things that I own, the lifestyle I lead. . . .

One of the most spiritually nourishing things I can do for myself is to "shed." To shed more and more things. . . . I have found, with some amount of surprise, that each time I let go of something, I experience a sense of peace; my roots go down deeper.

Carin Anderson, 2003

. . . I came across a study by a social scientist whose specialty is happiness. What he confirmed is that happiness is not a consumer good—not a pot of gold at the end of the rainbow. Rather, happiness lies in its pursuit, in the process of purposeful living.

David Yount, 2003

I was talking with Lillian Hall about the people from the US who come to Nicaragua under the ProNica Project. She told me that the US folk, especially the young people, are amazed to see that the impoverished Nicaraguan people are happy. "How could they be happy without things?" We should ask instead, "Are we happy with all our things?"

Mary Lord, 2004

Queries

Does the pace of my life leave me time to pursue those activities that nurture my soul, my family, my community, and the planet?

What helps me resist the urge to try to fill the spiritual emptiness I sometimes feel inside with busyness or consumer goods?

Do I pray for spiritual clarity before I take on a new activity or make a major purchase?

Practicing Peace in our Everyday Lives
with the Earth

But ask the beasts, and they will teach you;
the birds of the air, and they will tell you;
or the plants of the earth, and they will teach
  you,
and the fish of the sea will declare to you.

Job 12:7–8

Educator Jim Corbett spent years listening to the earth and its innumerable creatures as he rambled through the arid but beautiful Sonoran desert in Arizona, herding goats. Of his time following the flock through barren wilderness he wrote, "Leisure, solitude, dependence on uncontrolled natural rhythms, alert, concentration on present events, long nights devoted to quiet watching—little wonder that so many religions originated among herders and so many religious metaphors are pastoral."[15]

Jim's time among the wild plants and wandering animals of the desert not only deepened his relationship with God, it also opened his heart to the suffering of others. So in the 1980s when he learned that Central American refugees were fleeing for their lives from war and terror through the stark desert lands where he herded, he was led to organize assistance for them. He began by sending five hundred letters asking for help in forming "the new underground railroad," which became known as the Central American Sanctuary Movement. Working tirelessly and sometimes at great personal risk, Jim Corbett spent years helping refugees cross the border to reach Catholic and Protestant sanctuary churches in the United States and to find safe havens in Canada.[16]

Pastor Richard J. Foster talks about three great "books" that guide our lives: the book of scripture, the book of experience, and the

book of nature.[17] And since these three books are based on continuing revelation, just as God once spoke to Moses through a burning bush and sent Noah an olive branch in the beak of a dove, God
is still speaking to us through sparrows singing on the sidewalk,
trees nodding in the wind, and shafts of light breaking through
dark thunderheads. It is not the birds, trees, and clouds themselves,
but the sense of God's presence they invoke that speaks to us of
wonder, compassion, and transformation. But we must watch
patiently and listen prayerfully if we are to hear God's message of
peace whispering to us through the voices, both grand and humble,
of the mountains, soil, rocks, plants, and animals great and small.

Creation declares the glory of God to us in myriad ways, and we
each hear its voice differently. The voice may come through surg-
ing rivers or crashing seas, through the intricate beauty of a rose
or the delicacy of a dandelion gone to seed, through the soaring
majesty of an eagle or the bouncing flight of the goldfinch; it may
come through scowling gray-green thunderheads or through a
flaming pink sunset sky. Whatever the source, the silent voice
addresses us and comes to help us tremble in eager amazement
before the Creator. . . . All creation does tell of the glory of God,
and we will advance in our spiritual journey if we will listen.
"Earth's crammed with heaven, And every common bush afire
with God; But only the one who sees, takes off their shoes,"
wrote [poet] Elizabeth Barrett Browning.

Howard R. Macy, 1988

But beauty seen is never lost,
　　God's colors all are fast;
The glory of this sunset heaven
　　Into my soul has passed
A sense of gladness unconfined
　　To mortal date or clime;

As the soul liveth, it shall live
Beyond the years of time.

John Greenleaf Whittier, 1876

I read each misty mountain sign,
I know the voice of wave and pine,
And I am yours, and ye are mine.

Life's burdens fall, its discords cease,
I lapse into the glad release
Of Nature's own exceeding peace.

John Greenleaf Whittier, 1853

My walking has always been in search of water, and not so much the gathered and stored water of the lake, but the fresh-running water, the living, laughing, life-giving water of the little streams. I like to see how they go, where the water comes from and how it runs, through the meadows, over the rocks, down the falls. The woods and the water have re-joined me with parts of myself I had not forgotten altogether, but had scarcely really touched for this long time. They have helped to bring me closer to the springs of living water deep within, to tears, and to the knowledge that must be always flowing, giving, moving on, even before we know that it is ours. We cannot catch it, but must let it flow, over the water-fall, over the rocks, down the stream, in the sure knowing that the stream will never cease from flowing, flowing.

Frances Irene Taber, 1997

Walking through the woods at night, I put out my flashlight and sat down upon a big flat rock, determined to become acquainted with the dark. . . . Crickets chirped and a faint drone of insect airplanes passed my ear. My eyes caught the steady light of a few bright stars as I peered up past the treetops to the infinity beyond. . . .

My heart swelled in gratitude as I knew that whatever this life continuum was, I lived it with a love I had never known before. I felt it to be beneficence incarnate. As the silence deepened and the peace grew more profound, I seemed to be surrounded and nourished by infinite love. The leaves of the trees were whispering that they loved me. The air caressed me as it touched my skin. The frog sonata became a tender love song; and I felt that right here, on this rock, I belonged—yesterday, today and forever. Here was home. Here I was safe in the boundless care of a father and mother whom I could not see, but could only feel—a father and mother whose presence I could never escape, whose love would enfold me always, everywhere.

Lawrence S. Aspey, 1991

Stop for a moment beside a young cedar to listen
and breathe in the life swarming around you.
A soft breeze brushes your cheek;
you can *feel* the silence.
For a thrumming instant you are one with it—
life within and among this life.
At such moments, we don't simply believe,
we *know* that we are woven into the mat of interdependent life.
This is not sacred belief;
it is sacred knowledge.
We know in our bones that we are an intimate part of all life,
not simply what surrounds us in the present,
but of all life in all time.
The oxygen we breathe,
the nourishment from the plants beside us,
the elements beneath our feet—
all come to us from the most distant past
and will endure in some form into the unimaginable future.
We are ineluctably a part of all space and time.

Laurent A. Parks Daloz, 2004

. . . Some Thing that moves among the stars,
And holds the cosmos in a web of law,
Moves too in me; a hunger, a quick thaw

Of soul that liquefies the ancient bars,
As I, a member of creation, sing
The burning oneness binding everything.

Kenneth E. Boulding, 1945

It would go a great way to caution and direct people in their use of the world if we were better studied and knowledgeable about the creation of it. For how could we find the confidence to abuse it, while we should see the Great Creator stare us in the face, in all and every part thereof?

William Penn, 1692

In our bodies, as in the soil-body of the earth, remnants of the most ancient life forms are virtually immortal: bacteria, mitochondria, and other tiny organisms, subsumed by our cells and our selves. . . . Certainly we grossly abuse the soil's body—and therefore our own. Each year for instance, soil erosion in the U.S. exceeds soil formation by a factor of at least ten; and as soil degrades it contributes carbon dioxide to global warming. Each year up to half the nitrogen we pour onto our farms, lawns and golf courses leaches into ground and surface water as nitrate— toxic in high levels to humans and countless other organisms—or leaks into the air as nitrous oxide, a greenhouse gas hundreds of times more potent than CO_2 and a contributor to acid rain. . . . We begin to grasp, however, that whatever fouls the soil also fouls the human body.

Tom Small, 2004

Let us remember during these times that
"Peace on Earth" includes "Peace with Earth."

Ruah Swennerfelt, 2006

It is painful in the extreme to think of the possibility that things we have been taught to do for ourselves, for our loved ones, and for society as a whole are part of the problem. . . . Thomas Berry (Catholic priest and scholar) cautions against thinking that our environmental problems are caused by evil people. While there will always be evil . . . our predicament comes as a result of a great many good people who have been doing a very good job of what they are expected to do.

Ed Darby, Keith Helmuth, and Margaret Mansfield, 2004

Many people might throw up their hands in despair when faced with the enormity of the challenges facing us in cleaning up our environment and restoring the air. As Christians, we know that this is never an option. Perhaps instead we should lift up our hands in thanksgiving on this [day]. For we believe in a God who does not choose to leave us. Instead the Holy Spirit calls us to repentance, to a change of mind and heart—and lifestyle—for the sake of God's ravaged creation, the very creation that God once declared "very good." As the Spirit of God moves across our hearts, our own spirit is renewed from within, in a revival of faith and love. All that we do, in loving care of God's children and God's suffering world, we do in fidelity to the Creator, as a witness to the Commonwealth God proclaimed.

Ruah Swennerfelt, 2004

Queries

What have I learned from listening to God in the earth, rocks, trees, water, and animals? How has this learning affected or changed my life?

In what ways does my daily life exemplify, reflect, or belie my respect for the oneness of Creation and my care for the environment? [18]

Am I willing to change the way I live and make sacrifices in my lifestyle in order to preserve the earth, air, and water for future generations? What changes am I willing to make now?

Practicing Peace in our Everyday Lives
with Beauty, Joy, and Gratitude

For you shall go out in joy,
and be led forth in peace;
the mountains and the hills before you
shall break forth into singing,
and all the trees of the field shall clap their
hands.

Isaiah 55:12

On September 10, 2002, world-renowned Israeli pianist and conductor Daniel Barenboim defied his government's travel ban by crossing into the West Bank under diplomatic escort to perform at the Friends School in Ramallah. He took this risk because he believed deeply that the beauty of his music could help Palestinian school-children see Israelis in new ways.

When Daniel arrived at the school, which has maintained a calming, nonviolent presence in the region since 1889, the concert hall was already filled with excited Palestinian seventh- through twelfth-graders wearing school uniforms of blue and white striped shirts. They had been waiting expectantly for the great Israeli musician, and they applauded enthusiastically as Daniel took the stage. He began by playing Beethoven's "Moonlight Sonata," and the students listened with rapt delight. After he finished his concert, and the lively applause had subsided, he said: "What I can do is play music . . . for you, and maybe this way, in a very small way for these few moments, we are able to break down the hatred that is so much in the region."[19]

Daniel's concert at the Friends school brought him public condemnation and death threats at home, but the Spirit that rimmed his music with beauty that day furthered the cause of peace by opening the hearts of young Palestinians. At a master class he offered after the concert, Nadia Avouri, one of the students who performed for him, said, "Music breaks all barriers; I don't look at him as a Jewish person or an Israeli person. I look at him as a musician."[20] In subsequent years Daniel has followed up this initial concert by creating an ongoing fund to provide instruments for the Friends School's music program.

Poet William Carlos Williams reflected on the absolute necessity for the wisdom that beauty imparts: "It is difficult to get the news from poems, yet men and women die miserably every day for lack of what is found there."[21] Beauty, joy, and gratitude have the spiritual strength to break through political barriers, transcend religious differences, and bring justice and peace to a world awaiting their penetrating truths and gentle solace.

First, I want to hear about beauty. I want to know what you love. I want to know what words of love have been written on your heart—how you could smile at the bold beauty of a solitary hedgerow campion [flower] in December; how your taste buds might find sweet delight in freshly dug early potatoes, the way your flesh glows in the summer sun. I will tell you one of my amazing delights—how I held my wife up, her arms clamped around my neck, and how I felt against my body the bulge in her belly slip downwards as our daughter came into the world. Love creates beauty. I want to know how you taste beauty, about the woods and beaches that you love; I want to know if God-resonant Bach harmonies lift the top off your head. I want to know how you suck life into your being and live it, feel it, like sharp air in the lungs on a frozen, moon-smiling, diamond-clear night, and how your chest opens to compass the Cosmos.

Adrian Rose, 1998

[Beauty] breaks through not only at a few highly organized points, it breaks through almost everywhere. Even the minutest things reveal it as well as do the sublimest things, like the stars. Whatever one sees through the microscope, a bit of mold, for example, is charged with beauty. Everything from a dewdrop to Mount Shasta is the bearer of beauty. And yet beauty has no function, no utility. Its value is intrinsic, not extrinsic. It is its own excuse for being. It greases no wheels, it bakes no puddings. It is a gift of sheer grace, a gratuitous largesse. It must imply behind things a Spirit that enjoys beauty for its own sake and that floods the world every-where with it. Wherever it can break through, it does break through, and our joy in it shows that we are in some sense kindred to the giver and revealer of it.

Rufus M. Jones, 1920

No eyes that have seen beauty,
ever lose their sight.

Jean Toomer, 1923

As I follow the path of my Spirit,
great Joy comes to me.
Because I see everything is necessary—indeed,
I am often permitted to see the meaning and the holiness in
    everything,
even that which we call evil and depraved.
When I am in tune,
everything is a miracle to me;
everything is a message bearer;
there is meaning in each moment;
every bush is a burning one;
every leaf is aflame;
every instant is from heaven—
guiding, wooing, instructing me,
leading me through my astonishing life.

Gene Knudsen Hoffman, 1975

I am inclined to think that joy is the motor,
the thing that keeps everything else going. . . .
Joy produces energy.
Joy makes us strong.

Richard J. Foster, 1978

When my grandchildren were small,
I found I could make them laugh
by rocking them back and forth on my knees
and then suddenly changing the rhythm.
So it is with us.
Joy is the edge between terror and security,
we don't let it in
and so God has to take us by surprise.

Barbara Cummings St. John, 1995

When my spirit is animated by my religion
and is aware of the inviolable Truth prevailing,
my heart dances for joy and gratitude
and sings the praise of God!
Every moment is a mystery.
Even this body of mine,
what a mystery it is,
whose heart is beating incessantly without my knowing,
and whose lungs breathe ceaselessly without my knowing!
This air is God's, the light is God's, we are God's.
I am living with all the universe,
and all the universe is living with me, in God.

Yukio Irie, 1957

Are there difficult things that you can laugh at?
Chances are if you can laugh at them,
it means that you have found a capacity to carry the difficulties
    with you
as you consider them and you try to understand them.

If there is conflict for which you have no humor at all and cannot
   bear humor,
it probably means that you do not have the capacity
to do this work with your most gracefulness.

John Calvi, 2003

Sometimes those days when the earth gives us its blessing it comes at
precisely the moment when the blessing seems to have been taken
away. They come at time of loss and uncertainty when it might seem
that we have no reason for thankfulness at all. A few years ago I went
to visit my doctor because of a rather frightening and violent pain
quite unlike anything I had ever known. . . . "We'll investigate the
worst possibilities first," he said and proceeded to make the necessary
arrangements for me to go into the hospital. It all happened so quickly that I was sure there must be something very seriously wrong. . . .

I walked out of his [office] feeling stunned. . . . Yet I walked out into the
street and it shone like the New Jerusalem. . . . Houses, shops, pave-
ments, bare winter trees, were all incredibly beautiful to me that morning.
Everything was transfigured. Even the fishmonger's smile, when he handed us two cod fillets, seemed beautiful and very precious, as if it was a gift.
In fact everything seemed to be an astonishing gift on that bleak morning
when I wondered whether I was being asked to give it all back again.

Jo Farrow, 1990

I step into the abyss of faith; out past logic, theology, and my
deepest need, desire, and efforts to stay warm and safe and comforted; out into what looks like an abyss because I can't see, feel,
touch, taste, or more than barely believe in God in that darkness.

"Thank you, God," I say. "Bless you for what I see but don't
understand. For what hurts. For all I've experienced and will
experience. Help me to let you, cold or warm, comforting or
frozen, into every room of my heart."

I feel the quiet that precedes peace. But I sense that I still haven't
gone far enough. Even this isn't honest enough. Suddenly,

unexpectedly, the last thing I thought I'd say is torn out of me. "Thank you for the destruction, God."

Julie Gochenour, 2003

Not at set hours of the day,
nor in set seasons of the year,
does my heart offer its prayer to Heaven.
But it utters its thanks for each sparkle of a child's eye . . .
for each kindly look of the aged,
for every sign of humanity's strength,
and for every noble word of wisdom.
The glorious sun and the melancholy moon call forth gratitude.
Often, at a beaming smile or the slightest nod of a passer-by,
have I taken off my hat in reverent prayer.
For words of tested friendship I bow my knees to God.
Every object of nature and every act of sympathy is an occasion of
      thanksgiving.

Inazo Nitobe, 1909

The gospel understood is
"glad tidings of great joy" to all people.
Are you making it so?
Are you doing your part to make it so?

Lucretia Mott, 1867

This is the word of the Lord God to you all, and a charge to you all in the presence of the living God: Be patterns, be examples in all countries, places, islands, nations, wherever you go, so that your carriage and life may preach among all sorts of people, and to them. Then you will come to walk cheerfully over the world, answering that of God in every one. Thereby you can be a blessing in them and make the witness of God in them bless you. Then you will be a sweet savor and a blessing to the Lord God.

George Fox, written from Launceston Jail, 1656

Queries

How does my experience of beauty through sight, sound, taste, smell or touch enhance my daily life?

When has beauty in music, art, or the earth jolted me out of my routine existence, and enabled me to see the world with new eyes?[22]

Do I live with a grateful heart? How do I express my gratitude?

Chapter 3

Practicing Peace through Difficult Times of

Suffering

Grief and Despair

Healing

Practicing Peace through Difficult Times of Suffering

My comfort in my suffering is this:
your promise preserves my life.

Psalm 119:50

Bob Philbrook lived with hope, even though he endured life-long suffering as a result of severely debilitating childhood polio. He spent many years isolated in institutions where he endured several polio-related operations that badly stunted his growth and left him crippled and dependent on crutches and leg braces for the rest of his life. However, reflecting on his childhood, he said,

> I discovered God as a child, when I was kept alone, away
> from other children. The only person I could talk to was God.
> And I just knew, I just simply knew, that not only was there a
> God, but that God paid attention to me, despite the miserable
> physical and lonely state I was in. My vision of God being
> there was so strong that it sort of gave me permission to do
> anything I wanted to do.[1]

God's promise to accompany and preserve him sustained Bob's faith that he could, in fact, accomplish any goal to which he aspired. And in spite of his numerous physical challenges, Bob had many remarkable accomplishments in his life: he owned and operated a successful jewelry store, became a competent airplane pilot, earned a reputation as an excellent auto mechanic, was an expert sailor, and played trumpet in a jazz band in his community. In addition he maintained a long, successful marriage and raised six sons.

Over the years, as Bob Philbrook learned to live with constant pain, his ongoing suffering deepened his sense of empathy and compassion for the poor. He made a courageous decision at mid-life and sold his jewelry business in order to begin a career of social service which included being a community organizer, a counselor for high-risk kids, a spokesperson for the homeless, an organizer of a homeless shelter network, and a founder of a welfare rights group that still meets thirty years later.[2]

There are no satisfactory historical, psychological, or theological explanations for why the innocent suffer.[3] And while suffering can extinguish hope and shrivel souls, it also has the power to expand our capacity for compassion and help us become "wounded healers," people whose brokenness is a source of healing for others and whose lives help bring about peace on earth.[4]

It is wrong to talk of suffering as always ennobling its victims
and it does a great disservice to many who have suffered much
to try to explain away its presence.
The world is full of innocent victims,
and talk of sin as the cause of suffering
has often in the past simply been a means
of oppressing the powerless and keeping them in their place. . . .

Harvey Gillman, 1997

. . . Those who suffer are often the best instruments of the Spirit,
not so much because of their moral attitude,
but because they learn to submit their own wills to a higher power.

Keith R. Maddock, 2005

During the six weeks when I was receiving high daily doses of radiation, I experienced my whole body, in fact my whole being in a state of continuous suffering. . . . I was weak and nauseated, hungry but unable to eat, and deeply depressed as a result of the helplessness I felt.

One day, all of this reached an unbearable pitch, and I found myself hunched miserably on a kitchen chair trying to choke down a dose of liquid pain medicine, fighting tears because crying itself was painful. I felt utterly sorry for myself, and it seemed that there was absolutely no point in being alive when things were this bad.

But, in the moment of having this thought, it occurred to me simply and immediately that my very helplessness was a unique and incredible opportunity. There was absolutely nothing I could do in that moment but let go and experience being alive—I was not responsible for imparting meaning to my life, for doing anything in the world, for proving anything to myself or anyone else. I was not, at that moment, capable of doing or being any of the things I'd always identified with; no label would fit, not even my name. And, paradoxically, this absence of identity and attachment filled me with a deeper sense of individuality. I felt myself as a "soul," flowing from God and returning to God. No aspect of my true self was lost, only an old, superficial skin was sloughed off. There was also that indescribable sense of a presence that went beyond myself—a perception of God as something or someone real and immediate, not human-like at all, but of an entirely "other" order of being. I experienced this in a flash of illumination, but in a deep yet familiar and almost ordinary certainty and trust.

Kirsten Backstrom, 2001

I was terrified I'd break down.
I did.
It didn't matter.

Rosalind M. Baker, 1986

Pleasure there certainly is none in sorrow, but instead blessedness abounds therein. If we accept it and gracefully bear it, its hidden meaning will become clear and we shall grow wiser for the pains we endure. In the mysterious chemistry of the spirit, pure crystals and beautiful can be formed from bitterest tears. Only, for such a chemical process there must needs be a catalytic action, which is called Divine grace. The uses we make of sorrow are the measure of our spiritual growth.

Inazo Nitobe, 1906

My eldest daughter, worn out by what she had endured [from the Nazis] for her convictions, died a very bitter death. . . . I was dismissed from my professorship in Kiel and imprisoned. My youngest son hid himself because he had been sentenced to be lynched. . . . When people have to go through really deep sorrow, when something of the fundamentals of their lives is destroyed, they feel as if they walk and live under a great glass bowl. They see and hear other people, but they seem separated from them by an intense pain that others, even the most sympathetic, cannot feel. But if love works its great miracle, it reaches through the invisible wall. You do not forget what you lost, but sometimes you think that now for the first time you feel the innermost reality and beauty of joy, the creative power which comes to you out of it. . . . Suffering and joy are in a miraculous way connected with each other in this world of God.

Emil Fuchs, 1949

I still can't understand the facts of temptation,
of famine, flood, disease and death,
with all the undeserved suffering that these bring.
I still find that my attempts to explain evil and wickedness
are far too facile to satisfy myself, let alone anyone else.
But I know that . . . God loves and suffers with us and for us;
because in spite of all that I don't understand
and don't pretend to understand,
I do know that love through my own experience.

Kathleen Lonsdale, 1962

My own experience and observation of others tell me that in a world of fallibility, violence, and indifference we should not be surprised that wounds come to us. . . .Woundedness is part of the human condition . . . .As Second Isaiah suggests, we can find beauty even among the ashes of our hopes and plans, if we have the courage not to retreat from pain or to be dominated by it.

Elizabeth Watson, 1976

I have found that no experience is a wasted one.
But when sorrow has come to me,
even if at the time I was unable to see the situation positively,
I could always look back and see its part in the whole pattern of
    my life;
I could discover that it had helped me to grow.
So in the end, "why me?" becomes "why not me?"

Diana Lampen, 1996

[A]lthough suffering is for us an evil,
it is not the ultimate evil.
God does not promise to save us *from* the suffering of the world,
but instead saves us in and even *through* that suffering.

Tom Gates, 1997

Our English word *suffer* comes from the Latin root *fer*, which means "to carry," or "to bear" (as in *ferry*); and the prefix meaning "to be under." To suffer is to carry or be under a burden, and suffering was not originally a synonym for pain, but rather conveyed a sense of *bearing* pain, of *bearing under* one's disease. Implied in this understanding is the notion that one should not aspire to escape suffering, but rather to suffer well, in the sense of bearing the pain or burden of one's disease in a noble and worthy manner. . . . If to suffer is to carry a burden, then we ought to take seriously the Apostle Paul's injunction that we "bear one another's burdens, and thus fulfill the law of Christ" (Galatians 6:2).

Tom Gates, 1998

A friend once said to me—
I do not know which of our afflictions
God intends that we overcome
And which God means for us to bear.
Neither do I know.
But this is certain:
Some I have overcome,
Some I continue to bear.

Jean Toomer, 1957

. . . Our pains are our share of the world's suffering. . . .
The holes in our hearts allow us to see more clearly,
and provide spaces for a deeper empathy to enter the world.
I can—we can—survive the holes in our hearts,
and even allow them to bring illumination.

Ann Y. Robinson, 2005

. . . I search for equilibrium, for a reduction of suffering, out of my own, profound, inner need. I do this for myself as much as for others. I feel it sometimes as agony, and weep, for no apparent reason. More usually it manifests as compassion, and sometimes simply as passion. . . .

To cure myself, to find health, I must work to alleviate those sources of dis-ease and misery in the world outside. In the doing of it, however successfully or not, and in joining with myriad others in this struggle, laughter joins with tears, creativity and hope dance once more. We become whole again.

Simon Fisher, 2004

Queries

What is the suffering I have overcome? What is the suffering I continue to bear?

When have I been able to make a blessing of the brokenness in my life? In what ways has my pain expanded my compassion for others who suffer?

Am I cultivating a spiritual discipline that will help me withstand the pain and devastation of personal suffering?

Practicing Peace
through Difficult Times of Grief and Despair

Be gracious to me, O Lord, for I am in distress;
my eye is wasted from grief, my soul and my
body also.
For my life is spent with sorrow, and my years
with sighing. . . .

Psalm 31:9–10

After the World Trade Center collapsed on September 11, 2001, a dirge from the families who lost loved ones in the twin towers rose from the ashes. The Potorti family was among those who lamented, because their oldest son, Jim, worked in an office located at the site where the first plane exploded into the buildings. After friends and relations searched hospitals, burn units, and crisis centers in vain, David, the Potorti's youngest son, realized that he needed to have the conversation with his parents he had been dreading. On hearing the news of her son's death, his mother doubled over in lamentation from pain too excruciating to bear. When she finally lifted her head, her first words were, "I don't want anyone to ever have to feel the pain that I feel now." David saw the Divine Spark shining through her compassion, and he describes "picking it up like an Olympic torch."

Even though they were weighed down with grief, the Potorti family could see that calls for vengeance would simply extend the violence. So David gave an interview to the local paper on behalf of the family and expressed their wish that "we should seek justice, but not at the expense of other innocent lives." The family then began receiving cards from strangers thanking them for David's compassionate statement. But the most memorable response came when the Potorti family left the church after Jim's memorial service. An older man wearing a Veteran of Foreign Wars uniform covered with medals approached

David and asked, "Are you the brother who wrote that statement in the paper?" David replied apprehensively, "Yes," not knowing what might come next. The vet put his hands on David's shoulders and said, "God spoke through you in what you said about justice."[5]

The loss of his brother on September 11 ignited David Potorti's faith, and he has continued to pass the torch of compassion he picked up from his mother. His response to Jim's death has been to become an organizer with the September Eleventh Families for Peaceful Tomorrows, a group composed of the family members whose loved ones died in the September 11 attacks and who encourage nonviolent methods of conflict resolution.

When we are individually or collectively shipwrecked by grief and flooded with despair, it is tempting to want to strike back at those who have hurt us. Grief is heavy, cold, lonely, and angry. It throbs, shrinks our horizons, and drains the color out of our world. But God is always hovering at the edges of our distress, offering to sit with us while we wait for the stormy waters of grief to recede. And as our despair ebbs, we may discover that God has worked through our grief to deepen our compassion and inspire us to greater empathy with others who suffer.

If ever there was a time for tears without, and grief of spirit within, this seems the season: when after such an expectation of Light and glory, of settlement and establishment in the things of God such thick darkness, such universal shame, such dreadful shatterings, have so apparently overtaken us, and are so likely daily more and more to overtake us. Not only our superstructure, but our very foundation is shaken; and when we have striven and tried to the utmost to settle again, we may be forced at length to confess, that there is no settling any more upon it, but we must come to a deeper bottom, or sink for ever.

Isaac Penington, 1650

There is something compelling about calling my spiritual life a journey to a deeper bottom. . . . Most of us have a myriad of experiences in which we found a deeper bottom. Every wound we have recovered from; every time our broken heart has been mended; every experience of grief and suffering we have risen out of— these are all deeper bottoms—all the work of grace.

Peter Crysdale, 2003

I want to know how often you weep, for whom and for what you weep. I want to know how you feel in your guts when you wake up every morning to a world always half an hour away from nuclear night. . . . I want to know how you mourn for the cancered green lungs of the planet, for the juicy greenness that is being sucked out of your very soul. I want you to look through the eyes of the East Timorese boy who is forced to watch as Indonesian soldiers torture his father to death, and just tell me how your bowels turn over. . . .

I don't want to hear the bone-dead words of testimonies. I don't want to hear entreaties to calmness and civic responsibility. . . . I want to know if you have sunk down the . . .well of despair to meet all the conceits of yourself and humanity, all the self-hating and world-hating violence which is nowhere else but in our own hearts, and yet how you find at the bottom the unborn, ever-bearing Spirit which shouts "Live!"

Adrian Rose, 1998

I grieve.
It is a dead, gray mass in the pit of my stomach.
A mass weighing more than I do.
A mass beneath which crushed hope strives to grow again.
But to no avail.
It is a cold, lifeless mass weighing me down,
sapping my energy,
causing me to drag my feet against the concrete of the sidewalk.
It is here inside me.

I don't occasionally leave it behind or stumble upon it again.
It sucks away the heat of my body,
the strength of my bones,
the life of my thoughts.
Sometimes it rises up and becomes bigger than I.

Bruce Bishop, 2001

If I could find a cave that I might get into,
where I might mourn out the remainder of my days in sorrow,
and see people no more,
I thought I could have been contented.
But it pleased the Lord to open the eyes of my understanding,
and to lead me by a way that I knew not,
and to begin the first day's work in my heart,
which was, "the spirit of the Lord moving upon the waters,
and dividing the light from the darkness."

Elizabeth Stirredge, 1691

. . . If we really allow [others] a glimpse of our inner world, will [they] think we are mad or bad, or have lost our faith. . . . Those who have been thrown off balance by the shock of bereavement or injury need to be reassured that being off-balance and in a state of trauma is not a reflection of their spiritual life. . . . Being in a dark place can never mean being in a place without God and being driven into the wilderness is an honorable occupation. It is the place in which we are prepared for service as healers of our society.

Jo Farrow, 1990

Bereavement then can either break us down
or break us open to receive increased life.
When it happens, there is a sense
in which we are helpless to help ourselves,
and only a patient and steady desire for renewal of life can open
    the way.

Damaris Parker-Rhodes, 1985

When we accept the unacceptable,
it has no more power over us.
We can move through and beyond the experience.

Elizabeth Watson, 1979

Death cannot conquer.
God teaches ever that love is supreme.
Good people do not die.
Their lives are as the tearing of the veil,
they show us something of that which is eternal. . . .

John Wilhelm Rowntree, 1905

They that love beyond the world
Cannot be separated by it.
Death cannot kill what never dies,
Nor can Spirits ever be divided
That love and live in the same Divine Principle,
The root and reward of their friendship.

William Penn, 1693

It has been said that "time heals all wounds."
The truth is that time does not heal anything.
Time merely passes.
It is what we do during the passing of time
that helps or hinders the healing process.

Jay Marshall, 1998

Sorrow cannot be fought and overcome;
it cannot be evaded or escaped;
it must be lived with.
Whether it be sorrow for our own loss
or sorrow for the world's pain,
we must learn how to shoulder the burden of it,
to carry it so that it does not break our stride

or sap the strength of those about us through their pity for our woe. . . .
Somehow we must learn not only to meet it with courage,
which is comparatively easy,
but to bear it with serenity,
which is more difficult,
being not a single act
but a way of living.

Elizabeth Janet Grey, 1942

Once when for long months sorrow had clamped tight my heart, it was a minor ecstasy that showed me that life might again hold joy for me. I woke in the morning to the sounds, I thought, of rain on the porch roof, but when I opened my eyes I saw that it was not raindrops making that soft and playful patter but locust blossoms falling from the tree above. For a fleeting second my cramped and stiff heart knew again the happiness that is of the universe and not of itself and its possessions, and like [the poet] Sara Teasdale, when in similar circumstances she heard the wood thrush through the dusk, "I snatched life back against my breast, and kissed it, scars and all."

Elizabeth Gray Vining, 1942

Queries

When have I felt shipwrecked by grief or despair? How did I experience God's presence or absence in my grieving?

Do I allow my grief and despair to surface so that it can be healed? How do I avoid cultivating my grief and despair?

What is helping me live with my grief about the state of the world? In what ways have grief and despair strengthened me or affected my commitment to practice peace?

Practicing Peace through Difficult Times of Healing

*God heals the brokenhearted
and binds up their wounds.*

Psalm 147:3

James Guilford went by the name of Justice during his incarceration at Norfolk Prison in Massachusetts. While in jail he became a Quaker, helped start a meeting for worship inside the walls, and worked in the prison as an Alternatives to Violence Project (AVP) trainer.

Before Justice handed out AVP certificates of completion, he often told a story about a father who had care of his young son on a morning when he needed to complete some important paperwork. The boy complained that he was tired of his toys and wanted something new to play with. The father, worried about finishing his work on time, found a magazine article that included a detailed picture of the earth, tore the picture into little pieces, and gave it to the boy as a puzzle. He made tiny pieces, hoping it would take his son a long time to assemble the blue and green scraps of paper.

The boy, however, walked into his father's study a short time later and proudly announced that he had finished the puzzle. The surprised father asked, "How can that be? You just started it a little while ago!" The boy explained that there had been a picture of a person on the other side of the page, and he confidently informed his father: "When you put the person together, you put the world together."[6]

Theologian Henri Nouwen wrote: "[Jesus'] appearance in our midst has made it undeniably clear that changing the human heart and changing human society are not separate tasks, but are as interconnected as the two beams of the cross."[7] The vertical path of personal healing and the horizontal path of social action are both God's efforts to heal our profoundly wounded world. And since we travel these paths both as individuals and as an interconnected people, whenever one of us is personally restored to health, or peace is reinstated anywhere in the world, we all move a step closer to the commonwealth of God on earth.

The seeds of tomorrow's wars grow in the soil of today's
unhealed traumas.
The seeds of tomorrow's peace grow in the soil of today's healing
and reconciliation.

From the mission statement of Trauma Healing and Reconciliation
Services (founded and run by Quakers), Burundi, 2000

Each and every one of us
must examine our behavior
and understand that
we are one of the reasons
why our country has not found peace.
What are we doing?
How can we make the changes we need in order to find peace?

Vanessa Julye, 2003

[T]he soul is an appropriate battlefield
upon which to begin the war against outward evils in the world.
More than this: if the battle remains unfought in any soul,
then in our unredeemed regions,
seeds of sin and death (fear, materialism, distraction)
lie as in an incubator,
from which they can spread abroad anew.

Brian Drayton, 2003

My life is not clear:
I have used soap and water,
Chemicals and fire
Generated by friction,

Mind upon mind,
Heart upon heart,
Will upon problems.
Still my life is unclear
God make me clear.

Jean Toomer, 1946

Some of us know how to make our living being angry. Some of us by being resentful, some by shutting down and trying to live tight. . . . To ask to be healed is an incredibly courageous thing, because we will then be taken into a world that we know not and we will be stretched and challenged to make our living in a new way, not off our pathologies, but from our health.

Parker J. Palmer, 2002

For unless a person's unconscious life
is involved in their redemption,
how little in them will be permanently altered,
how heavy will be the shadow they cast,
and how opaque they will be as a window
to transmit . . . grace to others.

Douglas Steere, 1982

One day I saw that we felt the same as our opposition. We just used different methods. We still wanted to win. We still wanted to change others so they'd be like us. We still denied we had anything in common with the enemy; indeed, we often denied we had enemies. We were trying to heal ourselves from the outside. We had great teachings and thought we could live them by reading and talking about them. We didn't understand that inner healing had to take place first. Recognizing this, I began to look for new routes to become inwardly nonviolent, non-judging, non-controlling. I sought ways to integrate what I knew in my head with my behavior.

Gene Knudsen Hoffman, 1990

There are two Rwandan proverbs that emphasize the importance of speaking out about one's pain: "The family that does not talk, dies" and "The man who is sick must tell the whole world." Traditionally Rwandans and Burundians talk about their losses and talk through their grief with family and neighbors. Broken trust and dismantled families have impeded that intuitive process of healing, but it is widely accepted in the cultures here as an important step in the journey toward healing.

From a 2006 description of the Healing and Rebuilding our Communities Project, a Quaker project that grew out of the genocide in Rwanda and Burundi during the 1990s

Maximilla Shombe . . . became ill with high fevers and delirium one week after her first child was born. . . . For most of a week, her fevers continued, and she fluctuated between quiet delirium and coma. . . . The first sign of mental improvement came when in her delirium she began to sing hymns—very loud, slightly off-key, and at all hours of the day and night. Although we welcomed any sign of recovery, this new development was nevertheless problematic, as Maximilla was cared for on a 12 bed ward, which with overflow patients and helping family members often slept 30 a night. . . . She must have had hundreds of songs in her repertoire, and although there were a few old favorites, mostly she seemed to delight in reaching back into the far recesses of her broken mind, coming forth with a new Swahili hymn for every occasion. . . .

As she gradually regained her mental faculties, she revealed to us a positively sweet singing voice, and her tranquil smile seemed to convey an inner joy at simply being alive. Her singing, which had been such a trial to others on the ward, was now a blessing to all who heard her. . . . Maximilla had a tremendous physical and spiritual resiliency, augmented by her primal desire to nurture her baby. I also wonder if somehow her singing might have unlocked otherwise hidden powers of healing that helped start her back down the road toward healing. One thing I do know: Maximilla gave new meaning to the words of the old hymn "How Can I Keep from Singing":

My life flows on in endless song, above earth's lamentation;
I hear the real though far off hymn that hails a new creation.
Through all the tumult and the strife I hear the music ringing;
It sounds an echo in my soul: how can I keep from singing.

Tom Gates, 1999

In addition to its many religious forms, healing also includes many arts and sciences. There is the art of listening, the art of smiling, the art of empathy, of knowing just what people need, and not rushing in to offer help that is not suitable. Then there is the healing that comes through prayer in its various forms, through the laying on of hands, through music and dance, painting and color, through communion with and understanding of the world of nature, and through friendship.

Jim Pym, 1990

Art thou in the Darkness?
Mind it not,
for if thou dost it will fill thee more,
but stand still and act not,
and wait in patience till Light arises out of Darkness to lead thee.
Art thou wounded in conscience?
Feed not there,
but abide in the Light which leads to Grace and Truth,
which teaches to deny,
and puts off the weight,
and removes the cause,
and brings saving health to Light.

James Nayler, 1659

Be still and cool in thy own mind and spirit from thy own thoughts, and then thou wilt feel the principle of God to turn thy mind to the Lord God, whereby thou wilt receive God's strength and power from whence life comes, to allay all tempests, against blusterings and storms.

George Fox, 1658

The resurrection, however literally or otherwise we interpret it, demonstrates the power of God to bring life out of brokenness; not just to take the hurt out of brokenness but to add something to the world. It helps us to sense the usefulness, the possible meaning in our suffering, and to turn it into a gift. The resurrection affirms me with my pain and my anger at what has happened. It does not take away my pain; it still hurts. But I sense that I am being transfigured; I am being enabled to begin again. . . .

S. Joycelyn Burnell, 1989

We must be changed and changing individuals
before we can expect to make a difference in the world.
One cannot hope to teach what one has not learned,
and one cannot expect to influence significantly beyond one's
    experience.
Authentic transformation always begins at home.
As William Penn said about early Friends,
"They were changed men [and women] themselves
before they went about to change others."

Paul Anderson, 1991

Thus, we reach out to others
not as people who have all the answers
but as those who know the experience of fear and hurt
and who are in the process of being healed.
We speak to others who disagree with us not in condemnation
but with eyes which ever look toward the Source of our healing.

Sandra Cronk, 1984

Out in front of us is the drama of people and of nations,
seething, struggling, laboring, dying.
Upon this tragic drama in these days
our eyes are all set in anxious watchfulness and in prayer.
But within the silences of the souls of people
an eternal drama is ever being enacted,
in these days as well as in others.
And on the outcome of this inner drama rests,
ultimately, the outer pageant of history.

Thomas, R. Kelly, 1939

Queries

When have I been healed physically, emotionally, or spiritually, and where was God in my experience of healing?

Am I willing to try to heal my pain by talking about it with others?

Given that the seeds of tomorrow's violence grow in the soil of today's unhealed pain and trauma, what is the unhealed pain or trauma in my life that needs to be healed?

Chapter 4

Practicing Peace with Others through

Equality in Race, Religion, and Gender

Conflict

Forgiveness

Trust

Practicing Peace with Others
through Equality in Race, Religion, and Gender

If any one says, "I love God,"
and hates their brother or sister,
they are liars;
for they who do not love their brothers and
* sisters*
whom they have seen,
cannot love God whom they have not seen.

1 John 4:20

After World War I, volunteers in Quaker work camps built houses and distributed relief supplies in Germany and Poland. They lightened their physically and emotionally challenging work by forming close, supportive teams and becoming friends with the people they served. When Gertrude Powicke, a young British volunteer working in a small cluster of Polish villages, became ill with typhus and died within twenty-four hours, both the volunteers and the villagers were stunned and overwhelmed by this sudden loss.

The cemetery for these villages was Roman Catholic, and canon law decreed that only members of that faith could be buried there. The work camp volunteers, therefore, had to dig a grave for their beloved friend just outside the cemetery's fence. Many of the villagers, including the local priest, had not wanted to break Church law, but they were deeply troubled that this faithful young woman could not be buried in consecrated ground. The morning after the burial, however, work camp volunteers awoke to discover that under the cover of night an anonymous group of people from the village had quietly expanded the cemetery fence so that it now included Gertrude's grave.[1]

We are all beloved brothers and sisters in God's eyes, and acknowledging this spiritual kinship increases our tolerance and respect for one another. Educator Douglas Steere once wrote that because God is always looking for ways to help us recognize one another as brothers and sisters, God is continually encouraging us to "extend our boundaries outward."[2]

~~~

. . . One universal God hath given being to us all; and that God hath not only made us all of one flesh, but hath also, without partiality, afforded us all the same sensations and endowed us all with the same faculties; and that however variable we may be in society or religion, however diversified in situation or color, we are all of the same family, and stand in the same relation to God.

Excerpt of a letter to Thomas Jefferson from African-American scientist Benjamin Bannaker, 1791

We have divided this world into a place where gender, culture and ethnicity are used as ways of identifying and categorizing us into separate groups. We use gender, race and ethnicity as a means to justify hurting one another. Classism, racism and sexism are all products of this separation. We need to remember that when a man oppresses a woman or a person of European descent oppresses a person of African descent that we are damaging each other. We should not only know, but feel, that if I hurt you, that I am hurting myself, and when I help you, I am helping myself.

Vanessa Julye, 2003

Racism is very much like alcoholism. The alcoholic doesn't choose or intend to be an alcoholic; neither you nor I choose or intend to be racists, or to benefit from a racist society. Both are things that happen to us, through no choice of our own, without our intent. The alcoholic is not a wicked, evil person; neither are you and I. . . . The illness of racism, like alcoholism, is not my fault;

but it is my responsibility. I didn't cause it, but I must and can control it.

In both cases—racism and alcoholism—the first step on the road to health is to acknowledge the reality, to stop making excuses, to stop denying it. We need to face the facts before we can cope with them. In both cases you're never fully cured; the alcoholic is always an alcoholic. And I really doubt, sadly, that those of us who grew up in a racist society can ever totally shed our unconscious racist attitudes. . . . We can choose [however] to work to end racism, and learn skills to do that.

Alison D. Oldham, 1984

As a country, the United States of America was established on racist practices. The history of our nation begins with robbing American Indians of their land and often times their lives. The next phase of the developing nation moves to the enslavement of the African people: "For decades, white Americans had boasted of their humble origins and their devotion to democracy and the common person; but they never meant to include Negroes, Indians, Asians, or other nonwhite peoples in the American Dream."[3] Racism is built into our institutions from our federal government down to our local churches.

Vanessa Julye, 2003

In 1833 Sarah Mapps Douglass, a black educator, moved from her home in Philadelphia to New York City to teach in a Girls' African School. She was lonely in the new city and she missed going to Quaker meeting with her mother, Grace Douglass. When she attended meeting in New York, however, no one spoke to her. She had been attending one month when on the way in to meeting a Friend asked her, "Does thee go out to house cleaning?" Sarah reported to a friend that she wept during the whole of the meeting, and for many succeeding Sabbaths, not so much for her own wounded pride but for sorrow that Friends could be so cruel.

Margaret Hope Bacon, 2003

One has to fight for justice for all. If I do not fight bigotry wherever it is, bigotry is thereby strengthened. And to the degree that it is strengthened, it will thereby have the power to turn on me.

Bayard Rustin, 1988

Racism is one of the great evils of our times—as evil as war itself. . . . The destructive nature of racism was made visible to the world when Hitler, acting on the theory of the inferiority of Jews and Eastern Europeans, invented Nazism—a system of segregation, exploitation, subjugation, and brutal physical atrocities which shocked the world. War resulted. Quaker pacifists rightly objected to our governments' participation in the war. But was our objection as firmly spoken to the underlying causes of the war?—to the glaring examples of racism as practiced in Nazi Germany. And to the insidious practices of racism in Asia, Africa, Latin America, the West Indies, and the United States—practices in which we all have shared! It was these pervasive practices of racism everywhere that lent support to the Master Race theory of the Nazis and Fascists, and that led to the most destructive war in the long history of violence.

Barrington Dunbar, 1969

What was my horror . . . on March 30, 1942, to see signs on all the telephone poles in San Francisco stating that all persons of Japanese ancestry were required to leave the area before the end of the month. It was a shocking reminder that what had happened in Nazi Germany could also happen in democratic America. It was a bitter disillusionment, and it reminded me of our trip to Germany in 1936. Frank and I and three of our children had rented bicycles in Munich and had gone for a trip through the Bavarian Tyrol and saw signs in every village: "Hier sind Juden nicht Gewunscht." (Here Jews are not wanted). . . .

Josephine Duveneck, 1978

I don't believe personally that God has a denomination. Religion has unfortunately divided us,

but Spirit unites us. . . .
It is so important that we trust the spirit,
and to hear it speak to each and every one of us,
whether we be a Muslim, or whether we be a Jew,
or whether we be a Christian, or whether we be a Sikh.

Deborah Saunders, 2004

The humble, meek, merciful, just, pious and
devout souls are everywhere of one religion;
and when death has taken off the mask,
they will know one another
through the diverse liveries they wear here that makes them strangers.

William Penn, 1693

God hath made us all of one blood
to dwell upon the face of the earth.
We are all of one blood,
all the workmanship of one creator.

William Bayly, 1662

Those that speak against the power of the Lord, and the Spirit of
the Lord speaking in a woman, simply by reason of her sex or
because she is a woman, not regarding the Seed, the Spirit, and
power that speaks in her: such speak against Christ and his Church.

Margaret Fell, 1666

. . . The [Swedish] school board wanted to raise [Emilia
Fogelklou's] salary . . . [by] an increase of 50%. . . . But the raise
was intended as an exception to the rule and not as a general
principle for women teachers with her qualifications. Fogelklou
found this unacceptable. She could not bargain with her belief in
equal rights for women—and refused the offer. So she kept her
ridiculously low pay, while a less qualified male teacher received
almost double the salary. Emilia Fogelklou's comment was that at

least she had given the gentlemen an opportunity to reflect on the matter, which they had not done before. "They think that I have done this not for my own sake but for 'women.' I think that I have done it as much for the men."

Malin Bergman Andrews, 2004

The concept that we are all one is essential to the Christian message while the fact that we all have certain characteristics that distinguish us from our fellows is superficial. I do not mean to play down the importance of individual human qualities or the importance of each one's cultural background. I am proud of my Mexican culture, but I refuse to be bound by it! It seems that in our day we put too much of our energy into the expression of cultural uniqueness, instead of seeking for those elements in all cultures that can unite us. Christ brought to our world a sanity that, if followed, would liberate us from the dungeons of the separatist philosophy that has overtaken our age and would move us toward the great goal of one world, one humanity.

Elizabeth Loza Newby, 1977

Dear People of China,
Men and women with your patient faces,
Little children with your bright eyes,
How could I not love you? . . .

Of course there are many differences between us.
The traditions of our countries are different.
There are differences in our features,
And in our languages and religions.
But how much more we are alike!
Alike we are born to suffer.
We laugh and we cry as only humans can do.

Shall we be divided by ideologies?
No. No. We shall not be so.
Of course, "coexistence" has great difficulties.
Even those who have a common country,

who speak the same language, profess the same religion—
even such do not find mutual understanding, mutual trust too easy.
Yet the greatest barriers are not insuperable.
Let us strive to learn to live together. . . .

Emily Greene Balch, 1955—Printed in the Christian Science Monitor
just after her eighty-eighth birthday. Pearl Buck
sent one hundred copies to China.

It is the not-me in thee
that makes thee precious to me.

Old Quaker proverb worn on a pendant by Rachel Davis Dubois
(1892–1993), Hugh Barbour et al., 1995

We must be the first, the biggest, the best. Our world is not kind
to losers. Men's domination of women, white people's domination
of people of color, rich domination of poor and adult domination
of children all come from our hierarchical conceptualization of
reality. Our fragmented view that there are gradations of worth
among people concentrates wealth and power in the hands of a
few and has impoverished and oppressed many. . . . Walt Whitman
put into words for me this nonhierarchical view of human relations: "Whoever degrades another degrades me, and whatever is
done or said returns at last to me. . . . I speak the pass-word
primeval, I give the sign of democracy, by God! I will accept nothing that all cannot have their counterpart of on the same terms."

Elizabeth Watson, 1991

Guided by the Light of God within us,
and recognizing that of God in others,
we can all learn to value our differences
in age, sex, physique, race and culture.
This enables mutual respect and self-respect to develop,
and it becomes possible for everyone to love one another as God
    loves us.

Meg Maslin, 1990

Queries

When have I stood up and spoken out against acts of discrimination toward others or myself? When have I colluded by remaining silent or laughing when someone makes a racist, sexist, or discriminatory comment or joke?

What am I doing to learn and practice the skills necessary to end racism and other forms of prejudice and discrimination?

How am I modeling for my children, or the youth I interact with, the importance of affirming the equality of all people, treating others with dignity and respect, and seeking to recognize and address that of God within every person? [4]

Practicing Peace with Others through Conflict

> *Hear what the Lord says:*
> *Arise, plead your case before the mountains,*
> *and let the hills hear your voice.*
> *Hear, you mountains,*
> *the controversy of the Lord,*
> *and you enduring foundations of the earth;*
> *for the Lord has a controversy with the people. . . .*
>
> *Micah 6:1–2*

Angelina Grimke knew she was initiating conflict when she agreed to present the 1838 Massachusetts Legislature with an anti-slavery petition signed by 20,000 women. It was the first time an American woman had been given permission to speak to a legislative body, and many were aghast at the prospect. The Council of Congregationalist Ministers went so far as to write a pastoral letter to all the churches in Massachusetts warning them about "dangerous anti-slavery females."[5] This roiling conflict drew hundreds of people to the State House in Boston to witness the historic event.

During Angelina's speech she said, "I stand before you as a moral being, and as a moral being I feel that I owe it to the suffering slave and to the deluded master, to my country and to the world to do all that I can to overturn a system of complicated crimes, built upon the broken hearts and prostrate bodies of my countrymen in chains and cemented by the blood, sweat and tears of my sisters in bonds." And about issues of slavery and women's rights she said: "Have women no country—no interest staked in public weal—no liabilities in common peril—no partnership in a nation's guilt and shame?"[6]

Angelina Grimke knew that social injustices do not change until they are publicly named and addressed. Therefore, even when she

143

was called "Devil-ina" in the press, she believed that the conflicts she instigated by speaking truth in a spirit of love were helping to manifest the Commonwealth of God on Earth.[7]

Peace does not mean tranquility,
and anger does not necessarily mean violence.
Indeed, peace is all about how we deal with conflict,
not how we avoid it when it's present.
Sometimes conflicts need to happen for individual and social
change to occur.

Quaker Peace and Social Witness, London Yearly Meeting, 2002

There is an Indian legend about a snake that was converted by a guru and swore never to bite another person. But the local villagers took advantage of this and stoned it. The snake, angry and disillusioned complained to the guru who answered: "But I never told you not to hiss." We, too, must hiss if we see people doing wrong to themselves and others, but to hiss does not mean to harm. This is part of the obligation to explain and to help others to understand what they are doing.

Adam Curle, 1978

Paul Cuffee (1759–1817) understood the importance of confronting and naming injustices. When he was refused clearance by the port collector at Norfolk, Virginia, on the grounds that he was African-American, he went directly to Washington, DC, and insisted on an opportunity to talk with President Madison. When he met with the president, it is reported that he spoke in plain Quaker speech saying, "James, I have been put to much trouble and have been abused. . . . I have come here for thy protection and have to ask thee to order thy collector for the port of Norfolk to clear me out for New Bedford, Massachusetts." The president, seeing that justice had been denied, granted him immediate clearance.

Based on information from Daisy Newman, 1972

Anger is an index of our discontent
that needs to be heeded and carefully channeled.
We should find the difficult middle way between uncontrolled
    anger,
which erupts in violence and oppression,
and suppressed anger,
which may result in silencing individuals to avoid confrontations,
ultimately amounting to a greater violence to all involved.

Baltimore Yearly Meeting, 1988

On this path I have learned about my own wrong responses to resentments great and small.

- The first wrong response is to suppress it and try to act as though I no longer have it. To suppress resentment does not get rid of it but allows it to work destructively at a much deeper level in my personality. The better way is to bring it up and honestly face it.

- The second wrong response is to express the negative feelings explosively. I can get temporary relief in my mind but this does not help as a long-term remedy. The better way is to face the root causes and deal with them.

- The third wrong way is to run away from the circumstances that caused the resentment. This is like avoiding the person who has caused you to be angry. It does not help at all. I learned that I need to bring the issue into the open and talk with the person, instead of nursing it in my mind.

Nursing an anger or resentment is like putting a Band-Aid on a boil, which only drives the poison further in. The best response is to bring the poison out of the wound for a complete healing, which means accepting that resentment is wrong even if it may seem justified. The Bible says: "Do not be overcome by evil, but overcome evil with good."

David Niyonzima, 2004

St. Augustine wrote, "Hope has two daughters: Anger and courage." . . . While anger can be a negative, destructive consuming force, it can also be the vital transforming spark that moves us out of our apathy. Perhaps the tempering factor is how we channel that anger, and whether it is sincerely motivated by love.

Helen Steven, 2005

William Bown (1735–1824) was a slave by birth who, when freed, became a Quaker, well-known for his honesty and careful speech when resolving conflicts. William had a wealthy European American neighbor who frequently took advantage of William's good nature by borrowing William's grindstone rather than buying one for himself. One day after this wealthy neighbor had once again borrowed the grindstone, he thanked William, who gave the conventional response that he was welcome.

However, William felt spiritually disquieted after his neighbor left because he realized that his response had been insincere. So he went to his neighbor, and explained that he had told an untruth. William said that he believed that his neighbor should purchase his own grindstone because he was better able than William to afford one.

Based on information from Kenneth Ives, 1986

Ungracious politics demonizes our opponents. Refusing to weigh their concerns and consider their point of view, we slander their motives and question their integrity. We create an atmosphere of distrust and hate. Whenever we attack individuals, rather than critique their ideas, we violate the principles of Jesus and perpetuate the battleground of politics.

Phillip Gulley and James Mulholland, 2004

We are too ready to blame people for differing with us upon the great moral questions, such as freedom, equality, peace, etc. But when we think how different from ours has been their whole life training, we should try to exercise the broadest charity of which we are capable, and if we cannot convince them that our way is best, trust them and ourselves to a higher power, with faith that all will yet be well.

We are not true peace people if we cannot feel kindly towards all. . . . We can counsel, but never condemn, lest, in the error of our weak, human judgment, the condemnation fall most heavily upon ourselves.

Albert H. Love, 1873

Apology can be scarier than conflict. The apologizer is exposed, without the armor of anger, and admits to imperfection and to needing the restored good-will of somebody who has good reason to withhold it. . . .

- Apologize soon . . . rifts widen with time. . . .

- Apply empathy sparely. Pressing kinship with someone you have injured may backfire. . . . Bargaining dilutes apology. Never tell somebody you only did "y" because he did "x" first or that you will meet them halfway. . . .

- Apology may be private, but offenses that result in loss of face call for public restitution. . . .

- Give excuses. . . . The bad name excuses get is undeserved. The injured person's confidence has been shaken, both in you and in themselves as a good judge of character and a person worthy of good treatment. . . . By putting offenses in a more reassuring perspective, excuses restore lost confidence.

- Prepare to repeat your apology. . . . Forgivness, unfortunately, may come in stages, and the reward of apologizing may be having to do it again.

Dee Birch Cameron, 2003

Reconciliation is, of course, the ultimate aim of peacemaking. It is a word of power and beauty which implied, etymologically, the re-establishment of a council; as though there had once been a council of humankind that had been fractured by our errors and ill-doings.

Adam Curle, 1981

Queries

When have I initiated conflict creatively and constructively in the service of seeking healing for my family, my community, or myself?

What criteria do I use for distinguishing constructive conflict from destructive conflict?

Am I careful to offer criticism only when I can speak out of love?

When I am wrong, do I persist in apologizing until the person I have harmed can hear me?

Practicing Peace with Others through Forgiveness

"Lord, how often shall my brother or sister sin against me, and I forgive them? As many as seven times?" Jesus said to him, "I do not say to you seven times, but seventy times seven."

Matthew 18:21–22

David Niyonzima was teaching at a Friends school in Burundi in 1993 when the genocidal clashes between Hutu and Tutsi occurred. During this time of wanton killing, soldiers and their collaborators suddenly appeared at the Friends school, and without warning, opened fire on him and his students, killing several and forcing everyone to flee for their lives. David, a Hutu, escaped and hid in an abandoned building for twenty-four hours before he was able to reach his parents' home, where he was reunited with his wife Felicity, a Tutsi.[8]

After hiding for a week, David and a friend tentatively returned to the disturbingly quiet school compound, where they were confronted with thousands of flies and the smell of decomposing bodies. He remembers that he simply "sat down and cried."[9] After burying his students, he sank into a deep depression over the enormity of this brutal crime.

Despairing, David was almost ready to ask God to take his life when he suddenly received an "outrageous" spiritual message that he was "to come to terms with what had happened" and offer forgiveness to the men who had perpetrated the massacre.[10] Stunned by this message, he struggled with whether Jesus really intended for him to take his message of forgoing vengeance literally. If so, did "these teachings really apply to such blatant evil as this?"[11]

A short time later David encountered a man on the street who had collaborated with the soldiers and been present at the massacre at the Friends school. Much to David's surprise, he found himself taking the man's hand and saying, "By God's power, I forgive you for your part in bringing the soldiers to kill our students." In that moment David experienced a sense of deep peace radiating throughout his body, and he realized that by choosing forgiveness over vengeance, he had mediated God's love into the world, and that Love had begun to set him free. He describes this encounter as a "turning point in my life, pulling me away from the spirit of revenge which has overwhelmed the people of Burundi, and turning me toward the spirit of forgiveness."[12]

Forgiveness does not mean forgetting or condoning what was done; it does mean seeking to release ourselves and others from the painful grip of the past. Fortunately, our release from the limiting clutch of history does not hinge on the offender's remorse or apology. Desmond Tutu, Chairman of South Africa's Truth and Reconciliation Commission said: "If the victim could forgive only when the culprit confessed, then the victim would be locked into the culprit's whim, locked into victimhood. . . ."[13]

David Niyonzima's life was transformed by forgiveness. He says, "My complete healing has taken longer, and in some ways continues today, but that day [when I forgave] put me on the right path."[14]

Forgiveness is a condition in which the sin of the past is not altered, nor its inevitable consequences changed.
Rather in forgiveness a fresh act is added to those of the past which restores the broken relationship and opens the way
for the one who forgives
and the one who is forgiven
to meet and communicate deeply with each other
in the present and in the future.
Thus, forgiveness heals the past,
though the scars remain and the consequences go on.

These keep the sinner humble.
But now the past can no longer throttle. . . .

Douglas Steere, 1962

Forgiveness is a miracle of grace whereby the offense no longer
 separates. . . .
It means that we will no longer use the offense to drive a wedge
 between us,
hurting and injuring one another.
Forgiveness means that the power of love that holds us together
is greater than the power of the offense that separates us.
That is forgiveness.
In forgiveness we are releasing our offenders
so that they are no longer bound to us . . .
freeing them to receive God's grace.

Richard J. Foster, 1992

It [the Divine Light] is the indestructible power in us
that is able to create from nothing,
able to make ways out of no way,
able to change what appears to be the natural order of things.
It is the power in us that can never be overcome
by the darkness of fear and hatred
or altered by the might or money of people.
It is the power in us where lies unfathomable capacity
to love and forgive even the most heinous of crimes.

Ayesha Clark-Halkin Imani, 1988

If we examine where hatred comes from, we find it is the result
of injuries suffered in the past. Once those injuries are forgiven,
hatred vanishes. I had particular difficulty with forgiving my own
mother. She was a difficult mother—mentally ill and badly neglected herself as a child by her own mentally ill mother. I spent
many years trying to understand and forgive. But I was unable to
forgive her for the injury I had felt as a child. Finally, out of

practicing peace 151

compassion for that injured child in me, I gave myself permission not to forgive. At that point I discovered that my mother was forgiven not by my effort, but by God. She is forgiven, but it was not "I" that had the power to do so, but God within me.

Anne Curo, 2003

My heart was heavy, for its trust had been
 Abused, its kindness answered with foul wrong;
So, turning gloomily from my fellow humans,
 One summer Sabbath day I strolled among
The green mounds of the village burial-place;
 Where, pondering how all human love and hate
 Find one sad level; and how, soon or late,
Wronged and wrongdoer, each with meekened face,
 And cold hands folded over a still heart,
Pass the green threshold of our common grave,
 Whither all footsteps tend, whence none depart,
Awed for myself, and pitying my race,
Our common sorrow, like a mighty wave,
Swept all my pride away, and trembling I forgave!

John Greenleaf Whittier, 1846

Forgiveness of someone who has wronged us is very difficult. Forgiving ourselves for our own transgressions is even more difficult. Forgiving life—for being what it is—is perhaps the most difficult of all.

Anne C. Highland, 2005

The call to forgiveness and restoration
is not only just a personal act,
but a communal act desired by God
to make God's Commonwealth visible in our world at this time.

Pam Ferguson, 2005

I was invited by the provincial governor to return to participate in ceremonies marking the 35th anniversary of the rebuilding of the [Lapland] province [after World War II]. . . . When it was over, the governor rose to thank us for coming and to bid us goodbye. He was, however, interrupted by the official representative from West Germany, who said he'd been ordered to come to Finland for the occasion, but had dreaded doing so because he was too aware that it was his country that was responsible for the destruction of Lapland 40 years earlier. He'd been part of the celebration for two days, and not once had there been even a passing reference to who had wrecked the province. The focus was on the heroic recovery. No one in the room, he said, could appreciate what this meant to him as a German. His voice broke, and with tears coming down his cheeks he thanked the Finns for their spirit of forgiveness. It was a beautiful moment, and for me the powerful, compelling, confirmation of the triumph of generosity over vindictiveness, a lesson above all others that a hateful world needs to learn.

Stephen G. Cary, 2003

Let us bring our faith to completion by acting in love. . . .
Through love we see impossibility as possibility.
Through love, we see the unachievable as the achievable.
With love, we break the ethnic, tribal, and racial barriers.
Love will cause us to repay good for evil.
It is because of love that we are able to forgive
even those who have killed our loved ones.

David Niyonzima and Lon Fendall, 2001

Queries

Are there people or situations that I am not yet prepared to forgive? Am I empathic with myself about my inability to forgive? Do I ask God to forgive those whom I am unable to forgive?

How well have I been able to forgive myself for my past behavior? Is my inability to forgive myself interfering with my ability to forgive others?

Do I pray that an act of forgiveness that today seems impossible for me may, one day, with God's help, become achievable?

Practicing Peace with Others through Trust

*You who dwell in the shelter of the Most High,
who abide in the shadow of the Almighty, will
say to God, "My refuge and my fortress; my
God, in whom I trust." For God will deliver
you from the snare of the fowler and from the
deadly pestilence; God will cover you with pin-
ions, and under God's wings you will find
refuge.*

Psalm 91:1–4

One summer morning in 1775, the tops of feathered headdress-
es became visible through the chinks in the logs and the open windows of a Quaker meeting house in upstate New York. Those
assembled in silent worship placed their trust in God, which
allowed them to stay calm and centered in prayer.

When the war party burst through the door with bows and arrows
drawn, they were taken aback by the worshippers' trusting attitudes. Friends did not carry weapons, so the war party was also puz-
zled by the absence of firearms. The chief caught the eye of
Zebulon Hoxie, an elder of the meeting, and gazed at him fiercely.
No words were spoken between the two men representing the two
great powers that dwell within each of our hearts—the power of the
warrior and the power of love. The chief, finally disarmed by the
love he felt reaching out to him through the worship, signaled the
warriors to put down their weapons and sit on the benches among
the worshippers. The reverent silence increased in solemnity and
power.

After worship, Zebulon invited the Native Americans to his home
for dinner. Through a translator, the chief explained that the war
party had planned to attack, but found they could not kill people

sitting unarmed and trusting the Great Spirit. The chief attached a white feather to the center of Zebulon Hoxie's roof and explained that this symbol of friendship would make the Quaker settlement safe from that time forward.[15]

By trusting in a Higher Power, the Native Americans and Quakers were able to create a peaceful refuge. But trusting God does not come easily for many of us. We are wary and try to make *understanding* God a prerequisite for *trusting* God. However, none of us is capable of understanding the mind of God, which is why, throughout scripture, God reminds us that it is trust rather than understanding that will lead us to the comfort and refuge awaiting us beneath God's wings.

May God forgive the child of dust,
who seeks to know,
where Faith should trust!

John Greenleaf Whittier, 1852

". . . I raise my hands aloft to God, that I might be held by God, just like a feather which has no weight of its own strength and lets itself be carried by the wind" (Hildegard of Bingen, 1098–1179 CE). These beautiful words by Hildegard of Bingen speak to my condition. . . . I want to be in such a state of surrender and trust in God that I am like a feather. But, for me, the image of effortless surrender is in reality not easily attained. As humans we are conditioned to rely on our own personal will. Our ego depends upon it and our culture instills it in us. But I am beginning to understand that it is only by letting go that we are empowered. We need to make space for the true inner strength, joy and peace and allow it to hold us, lift us up and carry us onward.

Doris Calder, 2002

. . . We make a curious affirmation of faith.
Against all evidence to the contrary—
innocent children who suffer and die,
nations rent for centuries by ethnic hatred,
the degradation of God's glory in creation,
the ubiquity of divorce, senseless natural disasters—
We affirm that God is good,
That the universe can be trusted.

Felicity Kelcourse, 2001

God is to be relied upon
but not predicted.

Brian Drayton, 2004

It is not hard, you find,
to trust the management of the universe,
and of all the outward creation, to the Lord.
Can your case then
be so much more complex and difficult than these,
that you need to be anxious or troubled
about God's management of you?

Hannah Whitall Smith, 1942

I needed to place my trust—
not in a particular person,
a particular relationship,
a particular situation—
But in life
(which is synonymous for me with God).
I needed to trust the process—
to welcome whatever happened to me
as though I'd prayed for it.

Gene Knudsen Hoffman, 1977

. . . The reliance on God that can sustain us is a sturdy knowing trust. It means resting in God in the face of despair, failure, the reality of evil, and not having easy answers to persistently perplexing questions. There is something akin to innocence in it, but it is innocence stripped of any Pollyanna notions about our world and our lives. . . .

Mature trust appears most clearly in the lives of those who have learned to rest in the midst of the storm. We see it in the cancer patient who remains at peace because she knows she is enveloped by God's love and power. We see it in those who endure persecution with serenity and joy. Often it is precisely those who have been stretched beyond their personal resources and who have faced life at its worst who have discovered best the truth of the psalmist's song, "In God alone there is rest for my soul" (Psalm 62:1).

Howard R. Macy, 1988

There is no safety like that of those who put their trust in God and in the practice of God's will. "In returning and rest shall ye be saved. In quietness and confidence shall be your strength. Then justice shall dwell in the wilderness, and righteousness in the fruitful field. And the work of righteousness shall be peace; and the effect of righteousness, quietness and confidence forever. And my people shall dwell in peaceable habitations and a safe dwelling and quiet resting places."

A.J. Muste, 1941

A Quaker seeking to trust is not deluding himself or herself
into thinking that bad people are good people;
they are merely looking for the goodness in bad people.
And that, they would say,
is precisely what God does with us all.

Harold Loukes, 1960

A [Rwandan] widow [during a trauma healing and reconciliation workshop] said, "I cannot talk about effects of trauma on me when I know that I am with released prisoners." Another widow stood up and said, "It is true that we passed through difficult times! We have lost our loved ones even! Days ago, I met with the relatives of those who killed my family. They came to my home and expressed how unhappy they are to see me without my husband and my two children. They deeply asked for forgiveness and I have forgiven them. Now, we are in the same choir in our church. . . ."

When we talked about the mistrust tree [an Alternatives to Violence exercise], participants expressed how the mistrust tree is real in their hearts and the consequences of such evil. They openly manifested their willingness to uproot that mistrust tree because, they said, it is the origin of all the horrible times they have passed through for generations. "We have to plant the trust tree in our hearts so that every Rwandan can eat its delicious fruits," they added.

Adrien Niyongabo, 2003,
from the African Great Lakes Peace Project which brings
Hutu and Tutsi together to heal and rebuild trust

The politics of eternity
does not require that we trust them [our enemies]. . . .
They require us to love them
and to trust God.

Study of International Conflict, prepared for the
American Friends Service Committee, 1955

. . . I have been asked many times
to take leaps I did not feel ready to do.
But when I've done that I've been held
and I have been an agent for God
in ways I never could have been
if I didn't trust and take that leap.

Jean-Marie P. Barch, 1998

There is no going back.
We are a pilgrim people
who must take to the road again,
learning as we go to sing a new song
and to trust the God
who is always bringing new things to birth.

Jo Farrow, 1990

Queries

Do I make understanding God a prerequisite for trusting God?

What helps me trust God and others, knowing that trust offers no guarantees or safety?

What criteria or process do I use to assess whether I am too trusting or not trusting enough?

Chapter 5

Practicing Peace in the Face of

Evil

Fear

Vengeance

Nationalism

War

Practicing Peace in the Face of Evil

Do not be overcome by evil,
but overcome evil with good.

Romans 12:21

Lucretia Mott grew up during the 1800s in a close Quaker community on Nantucket Island where she watched fishermen, farmers, shopkeepers, and housewives—people with no extraordinary power—working to overcome the evils of slavery, violence, and warfare. And through observing her community's efforts, she saw that ordinary people *can* resist and overcome evil through prayer, speaking out, and direct action.[1]

The lessons Lucretia learned as a child about using everyday means to confront evil inspired her later work as an abolitionist. In 1851 she and a group of women from the Philadelphia Female Anti-Slavery Society came to the aid of a group that included thirty-eight blacks and three whites, many unfairly arrested and imprisoned for resisting arrest as part of a complicated case involving runaway slaves.[2] Lucretia and her friends not only allied to provide the prisoners with warm clothing and moral support, they also developed an imaginative plan to get them acquitted.

The prosecution in the trial had to positively identify the defendants as those who had resisted arrest. On the day of the trial the defendants entered the courtroom for the first time, dressed alike and wearing red, white, and blue scarves around their necks. Lucretia and the women from the Philadelphia Female Anti-Slavery Society sat in the courtroom visitors' gallery, knitting furiously, and "they did not so much as glance at their protégés, but it was clear to the reporters that they were responsible for the appearance of the prisoners."[3] Since the defendants were wearing identical clothes, the witnesses for the prosecution could not positively identify any particular man, and the jury found them not guilty. The disgruntled judge claimed the jury's not-guilty decision was the fault of "meddlesome abolitionists" and "itinerant female agitators."[4]

Lucretia Mott and her friends overcame evil with good by using their imaginations and their knitting needles. We, too, can resist evil and affirm our humanity through resourceful, everyday means. We can learn the language and culture of those with whom our country is at war, express our concerns for peace in song and theatre, surprise our critics with expressions of love and acceptance, and organize innovative ways to call public attention to homelessness and racism in our local communities. Since no good is ever wasted, any imaginative, loving expressions we offer the world, no matter how small, will make a difference in overcoming evil and building the Commonwealth of God on Earth.

Evil cannot overcome evil,
and the end does not justify the means.
Rather, we are convinced that evil means corrupt good ends;
and we know with a terrible certainty . . .
that when we undertake to overcome evil with evil,
we ourselves tend to become the evil that we seek to overcome.

Study of International Conflict, prepared for the
American Friends Service Committee, 1955

We must move beyond the naïve but satisfying illusion
that "we" are good and "they" are evil—
that the devil always lives somewhere else:
now in Berlin and Tokyo; now in Moscow, Hanoi, and Beijing;
now on to Belgrade and Kabul; but never in Washington.
The devil lives in the hearts of all of God's children,
and until we take responsibility to try to lift up that which is good
in us

and cast out that which is bad,
the scourge of terrorism will continue to torment us.

Stephen G. Cary, 2002

As the myth grows wilder about the influence of the enemy on a
victim's affairs, it has a greater gap to fill in explaining how anybody could be so bad. The distinction between doing evil and
being evil is one of the first things to disappear. Assumptions
about an enemy's sanity also vanish. Already we are in the territory of "Great Satans," "madmen," "the Evildoers," but lesser
labels also do dehumanizing work. Soon the complex human
motives we generally recognize in ourselves seem to boil away in
others. The enemy ends up with only one motive, which must be
as venal as can be imagined.

Ron Mock, 2004

Those of us who live in the post-Holocaust, post-Hiroshima era
can no longer deceive ourselves that evil will disappear when people are better fed, housed, better educated, more rational or more
devout. We have to get wise to ourselves and learn to love rather
than reject the world within us. Otherwise we shall always need
enemies onto whom we can project all that we cannot accept in
ourselves. We know now that unless we do, it is likely that an
upright, well-educated, affluent, church-going . . . member of the
human race may press the button that extinguishes civilization.

Jo Farrow, 1990

The planning, design, construction and operation of this factory
of death [Birkenau] were obviously done by very educated and
skilled engineers and administrators. The director of Birkenau,
we learned, loved flowers and his children. These people were
"human." One could probably recognize "that of God" in them.
But they committed the most horrific acts of violence upon hundreds of thousands of innocent men, women, children and
babies. . . .

Now I understood that there were other forces latent, or active, in the human soul as well. The reality of the Holocaust, and of countless other horrors, was driven home to me. What kind of responsibility do we each have for such violence? In a different time and place, might I be capable of such killing? In my own time and place, do I turn away from the horrors I read or hear about in the news, trying to forget them because "I can't do anything about it?" And second, I began to understand what Hannah Ahrendt meant when she wrote about "the banality of evil." Evil does not always come dressed in an obvious, ugly costume. More often it masquerades in everyday clothes.

Bruce Birchard, 2004

I am fully persuaded that recognizing in ourselves and in others both that of God as well as the evil force in operation is the way to peace. When we ignore this, we open ourselves to unlimited destruction from within and from without. Goodness is gentle and waits to be invited and nurtured. Evil is brutal and forcefully invades our spirits, our minds and our bodies. When we are not deliberately nurturing holiness as the basis for goodness and as the means of resisting evil, we give a free hand to brutal forces to invade and snuff out the Light Within both in ourselves and in others.

Miriam Khamadi Were, 2002

Your soul is vulnerable,
and it is bound up with the world at large.
The human soul, your soul,
can be seen as a nexus,
a confluence or focus,
of forces tending both to your good and ill.
Some of the evils can be seen as external—
sources of fear, oppression, or distraction.
Others are apparently inward—
anger, self-indulgence, and so on.

Yet we are so constructed that we and our environment interpenetrate.
Inward and outward forces activate or counteract each other.

Brian Drayton, 1994

I tend to see a person as being overtaken by Evil
(or the Demonic) for some period of time,
instead of seeing the person him/herself as Evil.
The Demonic often arises in us
when we feel we have been violated by someone or some group.
A feeling of self-righteous indignation wells up in us
and tells us that whatever we do to hurt the villain is justified.
In my own experience that feeling is the surest sign
that I am possessed by the Demonic.

Chris Beach, 2002

The Quaker message is to love your enemies,
not to pretend they do not exist.
Fox called on Friends to "wrestle with the power of [evil]."
This means we have to accept the reality of evil
and with love resist it.

Paul Buckley, 2001

Quakers did not naïvely suppose
that human beings were only glancingly conversant with evil.
They harbored no illusions that their developing ideas
about nonviolence were unproblematical
and thus subject to abandonment
at the first sign of malignity in others.
They found too much evil within themselves for that.

Meredith Baldwin Weddle, 2001

I remember a conversation some years ago with a minister of
Calvinist persuasion who asked me to explain Quaker views. I
replied that Friends believe that alongside a person's immense

capacity for evil, there is an equal potential for good often referred to as "that of God" in every person. Rather than resort to violence Quakers appeal to people by word and deed, to heed inner promptings of the Spirit of God and do good rather than evil. The minister looked at me rather quizzically and said, "Don't you think you are in danger of underestimating the power and influence of evil with that approach?" "No," I replied, somewhat startled, "I don't think so." The crucifixion of Christ testifies to what may happen when one is steadfastly loyal to God's calling. There is no guarantee of safety or success in the conventional sense in this approach toward violence and a person's capacity for evil. However, the resurrection of Christ stands as God's testimony and promise that ultimately the way of sacrificial love will prevail over the powers of evil and darkness.

As I reflected further on that minister's question my mind turned to many scenes I witnessed and stories I was told during my two years of service with an AFSC medical team in Quang Ngai, Vietnam in the late 1960s. Our project was located six miles from My Lai [the site of a massacre by U.S. military forces]. We treated at least one survivor from that massacre. Vietnamese friends told me not only of that event but of five similar incidents perpetrated by American or Korean troops in our province alone. I saw children injured by NLF rockets which exploded near their orphanage. I treated patients in our rehabilitation center who had extremities blown off by land mines planted by both sides in that conflict. Do I underestimate the power and influence of evil? I think not.

Marjorie Nelson, 1994

When we feel separated from the Spirit, when we feel separated from each other, and from the earth and the universe of which we are a part, we are living in sin. Only when we feel separate from others can we hate them, kill them, oppress them, discriminate against them. Only as we feel separate from the earth and all life on it can we go on destroying it. This feeling of separateness is based upon ignorance. This I believe is the origin of evil: the ignorance of our connections to the Spirit, to all other people, and to the entire universe.

Bruce Birchard, 1997

The method of Jesus in dealing with evil was, in a word, the over-coming of evil with good. Desiring as he did not the punishment of wrong, nor the defense of right, as we use these terms, but the making right of one who is wrong, he exhibited a strange contrast with the methods of modern law, industry and politics. He was able to draw the line in both his teaching and conduct between rebuke and reviling, between judgment and censure. The present day methods of dealing with evil Jesus habitually eschews. They are forms of coercion, by law, by violence, by external moral authority, by propaganda. Jesus relied on forms of conversion, by rebuke, by persuasion, by individual and inward conviction, and by love.

Henry Joel Cadbury, 1922

I have seen bullies and oppressors have their way, presumably without challenge or accountability, and they do much harm. But I also have seen them ultimately fail—and their demise is often remarkably quick and complete. This has led me to believe, sin-cerely, that acts of evil and bullying do not long endure. This is a source of great hope. Gandhi once wrote, "When I despair, I remember that all through history the way of truth and love has always won. There have been tyrants and murderers and for a time they seem invincible but in the end, they always fall—think of it. ALWAYS."

Thomas Ewell, 2004

Queries

When have I overcome evil and affirmed my humanity through resourceful everyday means?

When have I failed to see evil in myself and then attributed it to others?

What helps me hold a dual vision of life that acknowledges both evil and goodness, without diminishing the power of either?

Practicing Peace in the Face of Fear

*Fear not, for I have redeemed you; I have
called you by name, you are mine. When you
pass through the waters I will be with you; and
through the rivers, they shall not overwhelm you
. . . . Because you are precious in my eyes, and
honored, and I love you. . . .*

Isaiah 43:1–4

During the 1700s, two Quaker brothers moved to a farming settlement where rising fear and hostility between the homesteaders and their Native American neighbors was escalating. Despite the potential for danger, the pacifist brothers walked to their fields every day without firearms, even though, at a certain point on the path, they often felt someone was watching them through the trees.

The non-Quaker settlers became increasingly fearful and armed themselves. They urged the brothers to do likewise. Their dire warnings finally made one of the brothers so anxious that he also decided to start carrying a gun. He did not intend to use the weapon, but he hoped the sight of it would frighten away any would-be attackers.

The first day he carried the gun to the fields he was killed in an ambush. His brother, who did not carry a weapon, returned from his fields unharmed. Friends later heard that the natives had been watching the brothers for some time, and when they saw one of them carrying a gun, they felt it indicated his willingness to use it against them.[5] So the gun, carried out of fear, instigated the violence that cost the fearful brother his life.

The Bible, Koran, and Torah all urge us to remember God's loving promise of accompaniment when we are fearful. Although our fears can sometimes be helpful, when they turn our hearts against others, make our minds rigid, and narrow our worldview, we risk becoming our fears. And when we become our fears we are more likely to strike back reactively, initiate new cycles of violence, and draw into our lives those things we fear most.

. . . We need to remember that all the great spiritual traditions,
when you boil them down, are saying one simple thing:
BE NOT AFRAID!
They don't say you can't have fear,
because we all have fears . . .
but they say you don't have to be your fears,
and you don't have to create a world in which
those fears dominate the conditions of many, many people.

Parker J. Palmer, 1990

Fear which lingers,
fear which lives on in us,
fear which does not prompt us to *wise remedial action*,
becomes engraved upon our hearts,
becomes an addiction, becomes an armor which encases us.
This fear guards and guides us and determines our actions.
It leads us directly toward that which we fear.

Gene Knudsen-Hoffman, 1982

Whenever I'm in conflict, afraid,
I contract physically, emotionally and spiritually. . . .
This is fear of losing power, or control,
fear of looking stupid,
fear of being or becoming a minority,
fear of change and the unknown,
fear of the dark,
and this contraction is like the tightening of a fist,
which can be used as a weapon quite involuntarily.

David Sargeant, 2001

Without being conscious of it,
I slip into being manipulated by fear.
Fear makes me act quickly instead of pausing and going within.
I react to life rather than responding to it.
Since fear prevents me from taking risks,
I seek situations that do not require me to change.
Fear eats away at my trust in my relationship with God.
I feel stagnated.

Elizabeth Ostrander Sutton, 1999

I think the principal reason for inactivity is fear. . . . There is a saying in Kirundi, "Ubwoba bunyaga ubugabo" (Fear steals away a person's willingness to resist evil). It is as if we put love and fear on a scale, and fear is heavier than love. There are people today who are afraid to say the right thing to those whom they call the wrong people, or to do the right thing at what they call the wrong time. There are no wrong people. Every individual is created in the image of God. And there is no such thing as the wrong time for a Christian to be obedient to God, whatever the consequences. Every time is an opportunity to do good. We must confess the times that we have let fear keep us from acting. We must let love for God and others overcome the fear that grips us.

David Niyonzima and Lon Fendall, 2001

Fear is a powerful emotion. Once enough Germans feared the Jews, hatred grew and the Holocaust became possible. On the Indian subcontinent, Hindu and Muslim fears of the other community led to the slaughter of millions of innocent people during Partition. When enough Serbs were persuaded to fear the Bosnian Muslims, the massacres could begin. Fanning the fears of terrorism and weapons of mass destruction—both of which are real— U.S. political leaders convinced enough people that the United States had to launch a pre-emptive war against Iraq to make the world safe from these threats.

Bruce Birchard, 2004

It is war as it is now that frightens us. Whether we live in the West or the East we know that these [nuclear] weapons, any day, might be thrown at us, and we should have only a few minutes warning. The lucky ones would be killed on the spot, in millions. The courage with which we accept these facts and go on living a civilized life is admirable in its way. We suppress our fear. But, of course, this doesn't do away with it. It works in the unconscious. It tends, if we are adults, to make us conservative, clinging for safety to what is familiar. If we are young, it tends to make us grab at a good time now, because we have no future. . . .

So our basic problem is how to conquer fear and to replace it by faith—that is, by confidence in our world and to trust one another, however different may be the form of their politics or the color of their skins. . . . But the problem of fear cannot be resolved by any scientific technology; nor yet by any political organization. For it is a problem in personal relations, and such problems are religious problems, and can only be solved by religious means.

John Macmurray, 1964

If a wild animal encounters a human being who is not afraid, it is much less likely to attack. There is a good physiological, psychological reason for that: the animal is under tension. If the other animal or human is also afraid, then there are two centers of tension in the situation, and once again you have to "take it out" on somebody. But if, in that situation, there is another being who is not afraid, that releases the tension. There is a lightning rod for it to flow out through. There is nothing for it to feed on and to make an explosion necessary. . . . There is only one way to get security. That is to stop being afraid. That is what Jesus was saying all the time: "Let not your heart be troubled."

A.J. Muste, 1941

Once, in 1942, more than ten years before Rosa Parks was arrested in Montgomery, Alabama, [Bayard Rustin] had been forcibly removed from a bus after refusing to move to the rear of the vehicle. The arresting officers, in spite of their threats, could not shake his composure. Finally, an exasperated station captain shouted at him, "——, you're supposed to be scared when you come in here!" Rustin's rejoinder was quick and sharp: "I am fortified by truth, justice, and Christ. . . . There is no need to fear."

Devon W. Carbado and Donald Weise, 2003

The love of God
has been poured into your hearts,
so let it banish all fear.

George Fox, 1678

I heard Mubarak Awad speak this spring. He's a Palestinian who founded the Center for Nonviolent action in Jerusalem until the Israelis deported him. One of his insights that I cherish is, "We Palestinians found that the enemy was not the Israelis. Our enemy was fear, fear that someone else could take away who we were, could take away our integrity." No one can take away our integrity if we are clear in it. There's a difference between defending ourselves by shouting, "I'm not what you say I am" to a hostile world or a hostile person, and simply saying, "This is who I am." You can't kill that truth. Our "enemy" is the fear that someone else can take away our inner truth. I know from my own experience that if I'm afraid of anything, that fear will block my perception of my own truth. This led me to think about a Bible verse I learned as a child, "Perfect love casts out fear."

Janet Hoffman, 1989

It is not the goal to get rid of fear,
that is not possible.
I am afraid of fear,
because when I am afraid,
I stop being myself.
So I try to embrace it,

enlarge around it.
I do not try to get rid of it.

Barbara Potter, 2001

My job was to be eliminated, and soon I would be unemployed. My mood darkened to match the night outside. . . . Twenty-five years later I still do not know where the words came from, but I recall writing them down on a paper napkin: *Without fear there could be no courage. Without courage there would be no hope. And without hope, life would not be worth living.*

Until that moment, I had never thought of myself as a courageous person. In fact, most of my thoughts about courage had focused on the times my courage had failed. But now I had glimpsed a mysterious relationship between fear and courage that I had never considered before. . . . For the first time in my life, I began to accept my fears as a natural part of living instead of trying to eliminate them by being perfectly courageous all the time. I was beginning to see courage and fear as "dancing partners" rather than either/or opposites.

Lyman Randall, 1999

We are stricken with the disease, fear, which grips us in paralyzing fascination. Our foreign and domestic policies are filled with fear. Our personal lives reflect it. Our churches, for the most part, evade it by neglecting the urgent relevance of their fearless gospel . . . that God acts for humanity's deliverance. . . .

Dan Wilson, 1951

Resurrection, to my mind, seems rather to do with overcoming fear—fear of failure, fear of ridicule, fear of death. "Death, where is thy sting?" It is a triumphant shout of defiance to the powers of oppression, that they can do their worst in a physical sense, but ultimately cannot crush the Spirit.

Helen Steven, 2005

Queries

What are my deepest fears for myself? My family? My country? The world? What helps me counter and contain my fears, so that they do not negatively affect or dominate my life?

When have I acted on my fears in self-defeating ways and brought into my life that which I feared most?

In what ways are my fears affecting my faith? What effect does my faith have on my fears?

What would I do if I were not afraid? [6]

Practicing Peace in the Face of Vengeance

Beloved, never avenge yourselves, but leave it to
the wrath of God;
for it is written, "vengeance is mine, I will
repay, says the Lord."

Romans 12:19

In 1998, Emma Hazel Harrison and Al Starr chose to forego vengeance when their vibrant fifteen-year-old grandson, Cerrone Hemingway, was killed by a bullet in a backyard in Boston while witnessing an argument over a gold chain.

Shortly after Cerrone's memorial service, Hazel attended another funeral where she happened to fall into conversation about her grandson's death with a woman she met after the service. The woman listened attentively, asked Hazel for details, and then quietly said: "I don't know how to tell you this, but my son has been arrested for your grandson's murder." When the impact of this stunning revelation sank in, instead of feeling repulsion and anger, Hazel looked into the woman's eyes and recognized that they had each lost loved ones to the same tragedy, one to death and one to prison. They cried, hugged one another, and began what has become an ongoing relationship of mutual support.[7]

Al, Cerrone's Quaker grandfather, directed his energies toward helping people affected by other kinds of trauma. Al reflects that their experience made "an automatic connection for us with those who suffer from violence and injustice everywhere, whether it be fellow survivors of murdered children in Boston, or victims of bombings in Iraq or Kosovo." He says that as a direct consequence of Cerrone's death, during the 1999 war in Kosovo, he had an undeniable leading, "where it was as though God was pointing directly at me, saying, You! . . . You help these people!"[8] Al then helped bring a traumatized three-generation family of seven from Kosovo and supported them as they began a new life in Boston.

Hazel and Al could have reacted to Cerrone's death by demanding vengeance. Instead, they responded to their deep loss with compassionate activism. Their activism, however, has not erased the pain of their grandson's death. As Hazel says, "You never get over something like that; it is always with you."[9] Hazel became even more active in her grandchildren's lives in an effort to help them avoid what happened to Cerrone. She also became involved in the Living After Murder Program, which once named her Activist of the Year.

Because vengeance is such a powerful and destructive emotion, the Bible cautions that only God, not humankind, can assume responsibility for carrying it out: "Vengeance is mine; I will repay, says the Lord." But when we forgo vengeance, like Emma Hazel Harrison and Al Starr, we can end a cycle of violence, heal some part of ourselves, and help restore the world to wholeness and peace.

A victory by violence means humiliation for the conquered.
They have to admit the winner's superiority for the moment,
but the conquered vows vengeance.
Their resentment seeks satisfaction as soon as possible.
Their original anger, repressed by circumstances,
becomes hatred and longs for revenge and retaliation.
They nurse their grudge.
Their sympathetic family or friends may make their case their own.
Perhaps a feud or vendetta develops.
There have been many instances of feuds lasting many generations.
International enmities in Europe have lasted for centuries.
Retaliation provokes counter-retaliation.
The original evil or damage is vastly multiplied
and absorbs an enormous amount of time and energy
diverted from useful occupations.

Richard B. Gregg, 1959

[In 1980, Lady Borton went to Malaysia to administer a refugee camp for Vietnamese boat people. One evening Malaysian guards brought new Vietnamese prisoners to the camp. The other refugees immediately attacked them, mistakenly thinking them to be communists. This is her account of what happened.]

On the beach there were men everywhere. Running, yelling. Fists flailing. They yanked the prisoners into the sea, beat them, kicked them. I stood on the beach, paralyzed with fear. Although I can swim, even in a wading pool with toddlers I'll cringe at the slightest splashing. But more men were racing past me, pouring into the sea; there was nothing to do but follow. I dashed to the group farthest out. Water swirled above my waist, everyone splashing flailing, the victims moaning. The men pushed [one particular] prisoner under the water and held him there while they beat, beat. Grabbing at arms, I elbowed the assailants aside and yanked the man from the sea bottom. . . . Blood dribbled from his head onto my shirt. We were standing in water above our waists and he was gasping and I was gasping and swinging my arms to keep away the men who darted at us. I dragged the bloodied man to the beach where I stood holding him up while the mob seethed around us. . . .

"Move on back now," I said in Vietnamese. "Move on back." But they're VC! The men protested. . . . The little boy named Vu, his mask-like face contorted, yanked my shirt. He hardly came to my waist. "They killed my father!" He yelled over the mob's angry shouts. "If you kill your brother," I answered, "whom will you live with?"

[Afterward] . . . I sat alone on a nearby cliff overlooking the water. The endless gray of the sea stretched on until it merged with an endlessly gray sky. . . . I felt like weeping, but instead I sat on the rocks and let the heaviness settle deeper within me. . . . Someone spoke my name. . . . Turning, I found the island's head monk hunkering on the rocks next to me. . . . "We must ask your forgiveness, he said, dipping again and again. We're not ourselves on Bidong. "None of us are," I said. "Its all right now.". . . We lapsed into silence. . . . Strangers stopped me all along the path back to the hospital. "The VC are cruel," they told me. "We are all cruel," I said.

Lady Borton, 1984

All his life, Jesus rejected the use of coercive and manipulative power as inconsistent with his ministry. Now, facing the threat of death, he continued to refuse coercive means to save himself. Instead he practiced love. He loved so completely that he accepted his own death rather than retaliate in bitterness against those who hated him. Beyond refusing to use outward means of retaliation, he refused to become even a psychological or emotional enemy of those who wished his death. He prayed to God to forgive them, since they did not know what they were doing.

Sandra Cronk, 1984

As a Christian and patriotic American may I raise one cry of protest in your columns against the orgy of hate in which the American press and public indulges. . . . Americans with insatiable lust for vengeance cry More! More! Every concession on the part of the enemy is counted as a mark of weakness and is made an excuse for more humiliating and unreasonable demands. While the war-weary people of Europe long for peace, we conceited newcomers into the fight prefer to sacrifice their youth and ours by the millions in order that we may dictate a peace to suit our insane hysteria. Surely it behooves us at this hour, when not retaliation for the past but assurance of a safer and saner international fellowship is the world's need, distinguishing justice and mercy from blind revenge, to keep ourselves in the mood of moderation and fair play. A peace on other terms or in any other spirit will be no peace at all, but the curse of the future.

From a letter by Henry Joel Cadbury, printed in the Philadelphia Ledger October 12, 1918, which resulted in anonymous death threats and his having to leave the faculty at Haverford College

This incident [September 11, 2001] casts seeds of hate upon the wind. Our natural response is to ingest these seeds and let them grow. Yet this draws us away from Christ and ultimately makes us less of who we are intended to be. Christ's challenge is to turn our attention and appetite to the often difficult words and example of Jesus: "Love your enemies, and pray for those who persecute you, that you may be children of God in Heaven." (Matthew 5:44-46) We urge each of us to resist the temptation to use nationalism, retaliation, or demonization of others to rebuild a false sense of security. Rather, let us discipline ourselves to find our true security in Christ, and be merciful to all as we have received mercy.

The pastors and leaders of Northwest Yearly Meeting, 2001

We are too ready to retaliate. . . .
Force may subdue,
but love gains.
And the one that forgives first,
wins the laurel.

William Penn, 1693

We can celebrate the growth of the Truth and Reconciliation movement around the world. Fifteen countries that have experienced grievous internal violence now have truth commissions. At last there seems to be a growing realization that cycles of vengeance and counter-vengeance can completely destroy the societies involved and must be stopped. There is a space, somewhere, between vengeance and forgiveness, where enemies can live together again and societies can begin to heal.

Elise Boulding, 2000

Restorative justice is based on the premise that the appropriate response to a crime requires much more than the delivery of a "just measure of pain" to individual offenders, which appears to have been the basis for much policy till lately. Restorative justice is more concerned with the preservation and restoration of relationships both at an individual level and at a community level.

Restorative justice views crime primarily as injury (rather than lawbreaking) and the purpose of justice as healing (rather than as punishment alone). It emphasizes the accountability of offenders to make amends for their actions and focuses on providing assistance and services to victims. Its objective is the successful reintegration of both victim and offender as productive members of safe communities.

Tim Newell, 2000

Queries

When have I been seriously harmed and resisted the temptation to take vengeance? How did the decision to resist vengeance affect my life or the lives of others?

What helps me see the Divine Spark in those who have done serious harm to me or those I love?

When have I taken revenge by being indignant, aloof, cold, withdrawn, or unsympathetic?

What actions can I take to help break the cycles of violence that occur when people in my family, workplace, faith community, town, or nation engage in vengeance?

Practicing Peace in the Face of Nationalism

Behold, the nations are like a drop from a
bucket,
and are accounted as dust on the scales. . . .
All the nations are as nothing before God. . . .

Isaiah 40:15–17

When the winds of nationalism swept across the country during World War I, college professor Emily Green Balch was among those who paid a significant price for remaining faithful to her pacifist religious convictions. A dedicated economics professor at Wellesley College, Emily did not believe that dissent equaled disloyalty, so she actively supported the antiwar efforts of her students, helped organize marches against the war, and gave lectures on peace. When the college demanded that she give up her antiwar activities, she refused on grounds of faith, and the college terminated her contract. In response to her firing, Emily wrote to the Wellesley Board of Trustees: "I find it so impossible to reconcile war with the truths of Jesus' teaching, that even now I am obliged to give up the happiness of full and unquestioned cooperation where the responsibility of choice is mine."[10]

Emily spent the rest of her life working to create international peace-building opportunities for women. She helped to organize the International Congress of Women, which convened at the Hague in 1915, and collaborated in assembling other forums that brought thousands of women into international politics for the first time.[11] She also encouraged women to form communities where they could support one another in their peacemaking activities, because she knew from personal experience that they would need one another's help to resist the pressures of nationalistic conformity. Emily became one of the founders of the Women's International League for Peace and Freedom (WILPF), which dedicated itself to

183

building pathways to peacemaking that are still followed today. She was WILPF's secretary from 1919 to 1922, became its honorary president in 1937, and for her visionary work was co-recipient of the Nobel Peace Prize in 1946.[12]

Emily Green Balch dedicated her life creating openings and organizations for practicing peace. As part of her visionary work, she encouraged people to look for God's universal and uniting truths that transcend nationalistic identities. She wrote:

> Friends, let us forget as far as we can, those things which divide us. . . . There are no superior races. There are no inferior races. Let us learn to think of ourselves as members of that great race which is the human race. Wherever we pass upon the earth, let us be at home.[13]

[M]y definition of patriotism—
is to help a great country become greater,
and more worthy of its dreams.

Stephen G. Cary, 2002

It is the truest patriot who benefits their own country without diminishing the welfare of another. For which reason, those who induce improvements in the administration of justice, in the maxims of governing, in the political constitution of the state, or those who extend and rectify the education, or in any other manner amend the moral or social condition of a people, possess incomparably higher claims to the praise of patriotism than multitudes of those who receive it from the popular voice. That patriotism which is manifested in political partisanship, is frequently of a very questionable kind.

Jonathan Dymond, 1829

To consider humankind otherwise than one family,
to think favors are peculiar to one nation and exclude others,
plainly supposes a [deep lack of] understanding.

John Woolman, 1756

. . . Poor are the patriots who can find no faults with their own
country;
for a self-righteous nation can never improve. . . .
"Love is blind":
but when blind love guides us in national affairs,
where will the nation land?

Inazo Nitobe, 1938

To live in that state of tension which enables us to be
at the same time critic and friend of government,
to study its workings sufficiently
to be able to help religious insight become political action,
remains part of our duty and call.
And withal and beyond all,
to maintain an abiding faith in the power of good to overcome evil,
to live in that way of loving service for which we all most deeply yearn:
nothing less than this kind of energetic commitment of our whole
    lives
can satisfy the inner sanctuary of the human spirit.

Clarence E. Pickett, 1953

Here is the dilemma. On the one hand, the nation state is an
important source of community, of personal identity, of highly
and rightly treasured values and history. It provides that environment of the homely and the familiar without which we feel hope-
lessly lost, alien, and almost literally at sea. On the other hand, by
its emotional immaturity in international relations and its inability
to develop what I have called mature conflict behavior, the
national state is a threat to the whole system of humankind; and,

if humankind is to be destroyed, it will be the national state that will be the instrument of its destruction.

Perhaps the most critical question of the age, therefore, is how can nationalism be redeemed and transformed from the destructive and enormously dangerous force, which it now is into that creative institution which it has the potential to become. As I see it, there are two paths to this redemption. One is through the development of adequate world institutions to control armaments and to establish a basic minimum world law. . . . The second . . . is a change in the image which nations have of themselves. . . .

Kenneth E. Boulding, 1966

Friends set definite limitations, however, to the authority of their rulers. More than once George Fox demanded of officers of the law whether they should obey God or the law, and warned the king to "hearken to God's voice" or he would be over-thrown.

New England Yearly Meeting of the Religious Society of Friends, 1950

Nations have not deemed themselves bound
by the [same] moral code as individuals are. . . .
In our personal lives no one maintains that
because one person is strong enough to murder another
they are therefore right to do it,
or their reason for desiring to do it is righteous.

A. Ruth Fry, 1943

In troubling times like these, I take comfort, even confidence, in knowing that God is in charge and will prevail. . . . God will bring down arrogant powerbrokers and strutting thugs, in God's wisdom, time and way. But I'm not so sure that this is good news if my nation's leaders are among the proud bullies and when lots of people around me are thumping their chests in approval.

Maybe you have to be a little careful about when you pray, "Thy Kingdom come, Thy will be done on earth. . . ." But it has come, and it will be done. I think I need to join Habakkuk, perplexed and faithful. Even if everything falls apart, he said, "Yet I will rejoice in the Lord . . . who is my strength; God makes my feet like the feet of a deer, and makes me tread upon the heights" (Habakkuk 3:18–19).

Howard R. Macy, 2003

Upon [the prophet] Jeremiah there fell the unique sorrow—the sorrow of the unpopular patriot. Sharing all the suffering of his fellow citizens in the ravages of war and siege, even to the extent of voluntary self denial, he must bear besides, the intolerable burden of an outcast, misunderstood and unheeded, maltreated and abused, and above all, falsely accused of disloyalty and treason.

Henry Joel Cadbury, 1918

We know, however, that we must not flee from the world; we cannot place ourselves outside the political life of our nation; nor must we seek to escape from the greater tension, which is threatening to tear the whole world asunder, but must consciously place ourselves in the midst of it. If it is not to lead to a catastrophe, there must be enough people entering into that spirit that makes all wars impossible.

Margarethe Lachmund, 1952

My impression upon being released from prison [as a political prisoner] was that I was entering yet another prison cell, the only difference being that it was a little larger. Sitting in the middle of this cell called "Korea," or "home," and watching the flow of history, my thoughts centered on the following: This flow of history does not stop merely with the changes of national boundaries. It is the beginning of a world revolution in which the structures of human society are basically changing. The world must become one nation. The view of the state must be revised. The age of the Great Powers has passed.

Sok Hon Ham, 1969

As members of a historic peace church we love our country and sincerely work for its highest welfare. True love for our country does not mean a hatred of others. It is our conviction that only the application of the principles of peace, love, justice, liberty, and international good-will will make for the highest welfare of our country; and the highest welfare of our country must harmonize with the highest welfare of humanity everywhere.

David Hartsough, 1959

Queries

How do I answer those who say that I have a patriotic duty to support my nation's policies and actions even when I believe they are morally wrong?

Do I pray regularly for our nation and its leaders, regardless of whether or not I support their current policies?

When have I experienced consequences for putting obedience to God before loyalty to my nation?

What am I doing to make my country a positive factor in the world—one that works for peace, justice, and the betterment of the world community?

Practicing Peace in the Face of War

And I will make for you a covenant on that day
with the beasts of the field, the birds of the air,
and the creeping things of the ground;
and I will abolish the bow, the sword
and war from the land;
and I will make you lie down in safety.

Hosea 2:18

During the War of 1812, David Mapps and his wife Grace lived in Little Egg Harbor, New Jersey. The Mapps, who were African American, ran a shipping company that included a large sixty-ton schooner. One day a politically powerful colonel named William Richards came to the harbor looking for David. The colonel, who owned a local iron forge with several military contracts, explained that he had important freight that needed to get to New York as quickly as possible. Since the Mapps' schooner was the only available ship on the river large enough to carry this load, he offered David a generous sum for the delivery.

When David inquired about the nature of the cargo, the colonel revealed that it was fifty tons of cannon shot. David, a pacifist, refused the commission, and the colonel was forced to look for other means of transportation. It was extremely risky for David to deny a request from an authority figure across racial lines. Nevertheless, over the centuries countless people like David Mapps have been willing to endure financial loss, community disdain, threats, harassment, imprisonment, and even death for their moral refusal to participate in warfare.[14]

Through the prophet Hosea, God has offered humanity a covenant to end all wars, which we have yet to accept. Therefore, when a cruel despot is toppled by warfare, many are inclined to say that the war was justified. The problem with this perspective is that it lacks imagination, ignores the growing number of successful nonviolent revolutions against formidable tyrants, ignites vengeance, defies God's commandment that we shall not kill, and ignores a crucial, haunting question that echoes down the corridors of time in the aftermath of each war: "*Could there have been another way?*"[15] Today, as genocide, terrorism, and nuclear and biological weapons of mass destruction grow ever more deadly, "Is there a better way?" has become a question we can no longer afford to ignore.

We do not rest our witness for peace on isolated [biblical] texts.
We find war by its sorry nature to be a contradiction
of the message, the spirit, the work, the life and the death of Jesus
    Christ.
We believe Christianity calls for a radical transformation . . .
for the building of a new social order.

Faith and Practice of the Religious Society of Friends of
Philadelphia and Vicinity, 1926

People accept wars
because they do not see the possibility
of any other pattern of human relationship.

Richard B. Gregg, 1959

E. Raymond Wilson, one of the founders of Friends Committee on National Legislation, is said to have commented: "If you open your tool box, and the only thing in it is a hammer, everything will look like a nail." . . . We don't spend one percent of [our federal budget]—not one percent of that—on peace. So every time we open our toolbox, the only thing, as a country, that we have are weapons. . . . If the only thing in your toolbox is a weapon, then the only thing you can think of to do is hit the nail. Everything will look like a nail.

Mary Lord, 2004

War is an immoral act
sanctioned by otherwise moral people.
Nations condone ruthlessness as a means to an end
and blame God, humanity, and the devil for their behavior.

Henry Joel Cadbury, 1940

What is war?
I believe that half the people that talk about war
have not the slightest idea of what it is.
In a short sentence it may be summed up
to be the combination and concentration of all the horrors, crimes,
and sufferings of which human nature is capable.

John Bright, 1853

"But War," says Erasmus,
"does more harm to the morals of humanity
than even to their property and persons." . . .
One of the most evil consequences of war is,
that it tends to render the heart of humankind callous
to the feelings and sentiments of humanity.

Jonathan Dymond, 1823

Then there was an American atrocity I witnessed. . . . We had hit
some Japanese planes in one battle, and their pilots parachuted
out over the task force. As a radar technician, I wore earphones
that were tuned into the gunnery circuits, and I could hear the
chief gunnery officer break into a paroxysm of rage and obscenity
while the 20- and 40- millimeter guns fired on the helpless para-
chutists. I knew some of those gunners, and I knew they were
perfectly decent men, and somehow I began to get the idea that
the real problem was not the Japanese but war itself, as an institution that could turn otherwise decent men to this.

Kale Williams, 1971

I noticed a young American soldier at an adjacent table with his head in his hands, weeping. I sat down beside him and asked if I could help. He looked up—I judged he was maybe 19—and between sobs and gulps of whiskey, he blurted out his story. He was a draftee, new to Vietnam, and that afternoon had flown his first combat mission on a helicopter gunship. On the way back to the base, they had crossed a "free fire" zone—alleged VC-occupied territory—where he was ordered to shoot anything that moved. A woman with a baby on her back was working in her [rice] paddy, and the poor lad had done as ordered—he killed both with a burst of fire. "I seen the kid fly six feet in the air and splash into the paddy. He was just a little guy. I killed them both. They never hurt me. . . . Mister, I killed them . . . I killed them . . . that little kid . . . my God, my God. . . ."

Stephen G. Cary, 2003

[Emilia Fogelklou] realized that psychologically the peace-effort had so much less to offer than war, which appealed to the heroic side of human nature. "[Soldiers] all go out to war *thinking* to *die for something*, rather than to kill."

Malin Bergman Andrews, 2004

Ideals are not preserved
by putting them into cold storage for a more propitious time.
It should be fundamental to all religions
that ideals are to be lived by.
The saddest words I think I have heard
were those scratched on the helmet of an American soldier,
a dead American soldier, in Vietnam:
"Born to love, trained to kill, bound to die."

Kathleen Lonsdale, 1976

. . . I care deeply for those, many of them idealistic young men and women, many of them "weekend warriors" who have joined the service out of motives of patriotism and the need to supplement their income, who are now in harm's way. . . . I can, and do pray for their safety. . . . I cannot pray only for one side in this war, however, as much as my love and care for my fellow Americans fills me. I have to pray for the parents and spouses and children of our adversaries, for the safety of those who are going out to kill or be killed on both sides. I cannot pray for victory; I can only pray for peace and pray to be shown how I can be an instrument of peace.

Paul A. Lacey, 2003

War almost never works. Even when it seems to, for a short time, or after a long struggle, it is with a horrific cost of life, and property, and treasure, and the fouling of the earth, and the killing of its creatures. Almost always, similar ends could have been achieved through negotiation or international way and peacekeeping, with far less cost.

In the end, even when war seems to work, as in World War II for the Allies, it is because of the quality of the peace that followed. In WWI the soldiers were just as brave, but the peace was an excuse for revenge, and it led in a generation to Hitler and another greater war.

Mary Lord, 2002

Expenditure for war and the preparation for war is the greatest single item of expenditure known to the Twentieth Century. . . . War is the most extreme luxury known to human beings.

Ham Sok Hon, 1979

. . . Public opinion once set in motion is not a cool moderating force. Mass media are all too easily utilized by irresponsible individuals or groups, to fan the mass emotions that supersede rational analysis. Fear and hatred may be necessary to sustain a nation fighting far-off battles, but they are not emotions that can continue to be controlled. Just how far we have already lost control is suggested by the shocking extent to which the appeal to hatred has become commercially and legislatively profitable in America.

Study of International Conflict, prepared for the American Friends Service Committee, 1955

It was not a pacifist, but Field Marshal Earl Haig himself, who said: "It is the business of the churches to make my business impossible." But making war impossible is not only the business of the churches. It is a task for people of all religions and of none.

John Andrew Story, 1973

Our world clings to military power as the source of its security. . . . Our reliance on the force of arms has become an idol
which usurps God's place in our everyday lives.
To rely on military power is to rely ultimately on self
and to misunderstand how God works in our midst.
This misunderstanding is not a new one.
Throughout biblical history the people had to learn and relearn that their strength lay in God's power and not in their own might.
Indeed, the Lord worked in unexpected ways
which over-turned the usual assumptions about the triumph of
    might.

Sandra Cronk, 1984

Universal and natural as is the fighting instinct in people,
fruitful as it has proved to be of noble sentiments . . .
it does not comprehend the whole person.
Beneath the instinct to fight there lurks a diviner instinct to love. . . .

Inazo Nitobe, 1900

It is very striking to find that Napoleon, whom we think of as a believer in nothing but military force, realized at last his mistake. In the far-away isolation of St. Helena, he wrote this fine confession: "Alexander, Caesar, Charlemagne and myself have founded

Empires. But on what did we rest the creation of our genius? Upon force! Jesus Christ alone founded His Empire on love; and at this hour millions of people would die for Him. . . .

"Now that I am at St. Helena alone, chained upon this rock, who fights and wins Empires for me? What an abyss between my deep misery and the eternal reign of Christ, who is proclaimed, loved, adored and whose reign is extending over all the earth!"

A. Ruth Fry, 1950

George [Fox] frequently makes the point that, while everyone has the light of God in them, many people hate that light, because it condemns their behavior. To George Fox, being a pacifist in a world of war is part of being a soldier in the spiritual—not carnal, not worldly—army of Christ, of fighting in the only war that matters—the Lamb's War, which is fought only on a spiritual level.

Martha Mangelsdorf, 2002

We utterly deny all outward wars and strife and fightings with outward weapons, for any end or under any pretence whatsoever. And this is our testimony to the whole world. The spirit of Christ, by which we are guided, is not changeable, so as once to command us from a thing as evil and again to move unto it; and we do certainly know, and so testify to the world, that the spirit of Christ, which leads us into all Truth, will never move us to fight any war against any person with outward weapons, neither for the commonwealth of Christ, nor for the commonwealths of this world.

George Fox and other Friends, 1660

Queries

What are my personal spiritual beliefs about warfare? Is war is a moral act? Can it sometimes be just? Is it sometimes necessary?

How can I witness to my spiritual beliefs about war without condemning or belittling those who see it differently?

How is my lifestyle—the choices I am making about work, money, and possessions—contributing to the causes of war?

Chapter 6

Practicing Peace in the World through

Visioning

Loving Enemies

Nonviolent Action

Pacifism and Conscientious Objection

Accepting the Costs of Witnessing

Patience and Endurance

Hope

Practicing Peace in the World through Visioning

Look among the nations, and see;
wonder and be astounded.
For I am doing a work in your days
that you would not believe if told.

Habakkuk 1:5

In seventeenth-century England, women were considered intellectually and spiritually inferior. Authorities therefore felt justified in jailing women who were led to preach. However, Quakers envisioned a world of equality where God intended women to have equal rights. According to historian Mary Garman, they "interpreted the success of women as ministers and leaders as evidence that God was restoring creation to its state of original wholeness."[1]

The best known of these groundbreaking Quaker women ministers was Margaret Fell. She preached, wrote tracts, traveled in ministry, raised nine children, oversaw a large household, and provided spiritual inspiration and organizational leadership for Friends around the world. Margaret was repeatedly jailed for preaching, but she persevered in living her vision that women could be ministers, and in 1666, she wrote the first known defense of women's ministry, titled *Women's Preaching Justified According to the Scriptures*.[2]

Margaret's vision of ministry also included nurturing the formation of women's meetings within the Society of Friends. These meetings endured over time and provided the organizational training which prepared eighteenth-, nineteenth-, and twentieth-century Quaker women to assume positions of leadership in social movements such as the struggle for religious freedom, the abolition of slavery, and women's suffrage.[3] So the visions of Margaret Fell and other early Friends bore fruit in the social commitments of the generations of Quaker women who followed.

Visions of peace are God's invitations to look beyond the material-ism, individualism, and violence of contemporary life as it is and see how life could be in God's peaceable commonwealth. It is through our visions that God invites us to enlarge our imaginations, see what is yet possible, and live into our dreams of a just and peaceful world.

Yahweh asks that we become again and again
a people who embody an alternative imagination
in the midst of,
and over against,
the prevailing,
inadequate consciousness
or conscious-less-ness of every age.

Sharon Daloz Parks, 1986

The prospects [for the abolition of war] look dim, as dim as the prospects for the free exercise of religion 400 years ago, as dim as the prospects for the abolition of slavery 200 years ago, as dim as the prospects for women's suffrage 100 years ago. But a saving remnant of our nation could brighten the prospects to make a world free of war and the threat of war. We are called not to despair. We are called not to wring our hands, but to live in a world that is now-but-not-yet, and living in a now-but-not-yet world is how we will construct a sustainable peace.

Joe Volk, 2005

The crucial thing about humans and their societies is not where they came from but where they are going. What is of even more significance about Abraham than the fact that he emigrated from Ur of the Chaldees is that there was no city, no society or com-munity for him to move into. . . . The fact is that Abraham "went out, not knowing whither he went." He was a fool and a gambler.

But he was not a little fool; rather he was a big one, whose foolishness consisted in taking on a Herculean task. . . .

Abraham went out looking for a city which existed—and yet had to be brought into existence. It was the perfect and holy city—which had to be built and whose "builder and maker is God." The creative movement in history is not from any city-which-is to another city-which-is. . . . What matters is the movement from the unreal, because unrealized, city-which-is to the city-which-is-to-be, which is more real because the potentiality of realization and completion remains.

A.J. Muste, 1962

We are called to an Abrahamic journey,
leaving the familiar to walk with God
as a stranger in a strange land,
always inviting and invoking
a commonwealth that is now and not yet,
about to become and already here.

Lloyd Lee Wilson, 1998

This [prophetic imagination] is the capacity to see what is yet possible under the power of God rather than yielding to cynicism and despair or to a status quo, which is death warmed over. It is the capacity to know deeply that seeing the possibility of reconciliation and of restoration is not merely lofty idealism or wishful thinking. . . . It is Jeremiah buying a field while he is in prison and the Babylonians are conquering his homeland, including the field. Someday people will once again buy fields and plant and harvest in this land, he says (Jeremiah 32). . . . It is to hold out the real possibility that the future of our lives in the real world need not be bound by the patterns and failures of the past, but that it can be creatively ordered and empowered by the sovereign God who is with us in love.

Howard R. Macy, 1996

When tempted by sanity—
to see things as they are and not more—
may we be drawn to the redemptive alternative,
to see things as they could be . . . and no less.

Paul Anderson, 1991

The churches have become one of the places where dreaming is
    kept alive.
They have sometimes been distorted into defending the status quo
but their birthright, our birthright, is prophecy and the
    commonwealth.
In the Bible, dreaming keeps alive God's hope for all of us.

Jonathan Dale, 1996

Put in the simplest possible terms, a peace culture is a culture that
promotes peaceable diversity. Such a culture includes lifeways, patterns of belief, values, behavior, and accompanying institutional
arrangements that promote mutual caring and well-being as well
as an equality that includes appreciation of difference, steward-
ship, and equitable sharing of the earth's resources among its
members and with all living beings. It offers mutual security for
humankind in all its diversity through a profound sense of species
identity as well as kinship with the living earth. There is no need
for violence. In other words, peaceableness is an action concept,
involving a constant shaping and reshaping of understandings, situations, and behaviors in a constantly changing lifeworld, to sustain well-being for all.

Elise Boulding, 2000

It is bound to be difficult trying to live by ideals for which
the slowly maturing world is not quite ready.
But it is the price that must be paid for prophetic vision
and it is a risk well worth taking.

Rufus M. Jones, 1927

practicing peace

Visionary experiences have a terrible cost attached to them. To be sensitized by the Holy Spirit, or really open to the Spirit in a way which transfigures the world and enables us to see it with new eyes, inevitably involves an equal sensitivity to the darkness and tragedy of human life. You can't have one without the other. There is no consciousness without pain, and total awareness is a crucial, some- times crucifying business. How could it be otherwise. . . .

Jo Farrow, 1990

For we do not create the peaceable commonwealth with our power. We enter into God's commonwealth which is emerging in our midst. With this understanding, despair cannot overwhelm us.

Sandra Cronk, 1984

A.J. Muste used to tell a story of some explorers shivering through the night. One stuck his head through the tent flaps and saw the faintest glow lining the Eastern horizon. "Morning's coming," he shouted. His companions saw only darkness, and derided and denied. "Nevertheless," A.J. would say in his own quiet way, "dawn came."

Pat Clark, 2004

[Quakers] thought it is a matter of a good deal of importance to have a body of people, even though it may be a small body, who will not surrender their ideal—their vision of advance—even in the face of the earthquake and the broken strata. It is worth something to have the lighted torch held high, when others have allowed the swirl of the storm to blow theirs out.

Rufus M. Jones, 1927

If any of us feel daunted, let us take heart.
Remember that the Commonwealth of God is within us—
and seek to reveal it.
Remember that Jesus also said, according to Thomas,

"The Commonwealth is spread upon the earth but ye see it not"—
let us seek to see it. . . .

Adam Curle, 1981

Queries

*What does my vision of the Commonwealth of God on Earth look like?
How are disputes settled, resources allocated, the environment protect-
ed, children educated, the elderly cared for, and health care provided?*

*In what ways am I already living into my vision of the
Commonwealth of God on Earth?*

*What new steps do I feel led to take toward living in the
Commonwealth of God on Earth?*

Practicing Peace in the World
through Loving Enemies

*You have heard that it was said, "You shall love
your neighbor and hate your enemy." But I say
to you, Love your enemies and pray for those who
persecute you, so that you may be the sons and
daughters of God who is in heaven; for God
makes the sun rise on the evil and on the good,
and sends rain on the just and on the unjust.*

Matthew 5:43–45

The Goffs were among the many Irish Quaker families during
the Rebellion of 1798 who practiced peace by offering medical
assistance in their homes to both loyalists *and* rebels. Although
both sides threatened them with death, these families steadfastly
refused to turn their patients over to military authorities. And
they tried to love both the loyalist and rebel soldiers who were
intimidating them, even as they condemned the violence they
were perpetrating.[4]

The unconditional love emanating from these families, who willingly put themselves at risk, convinced soldiers on both sides that
Quakers like the Goffs were simply practicing peace by extending
care to everyone in need. So, although journals from that period
record that both armies had scorched-earth policies, historian
Margaret Hirst wrote that because no known Friends' homes were
destroyed during the rebellion, "strangers passing the houses of
Friends and seeing them preserved with ruins on either hand would
frequently, without knowledge of the district, say they were
'Quaker houses.'"[5]

Only God can know the contents of a human heart, so the Irish
Quakers knew they could never fully comprehend what was impelling

the soldiers to acts of desperation and cruelty. They also knew from looking within themselves, that the capacity for evil is in us all, and so instead of passing judgment, they expressed loving kindness to those who found swords within their hearts and chose to use them.[6]

The challenge of loving those traditionally considered enemies lies at the heart of the Quaker peace testimony, because when we are able to extend our love, even to those who would frustrate, terrorize, or harm us, we bring God's grace of transformative love into our homes, communities, and a world weary of violence. The future of our planet may ultimately depend on our ability to enlarge our capacity for redemptive love and our willingness to extend that love even to those who threaten us.

No plea of necessity or of policy,
however urgent or peculiar,
can avail to release either individuals or nations
from the paramount allegiance which they owe unto God
who hath said "Love your enemies."

London Yearly Meeting, during the Crimean War, 1854

A theology of love is grounded in the realization that God loves our enemies as much as God loves us. And we are all created in the image of this God. We are all precious in God's sight. We are all children of God. This, more than any other idea, changes how we perceive others. It requires us to call every man and every woman by the names that make murder nearly impossible—brother and sister.

Phillip Gulley and James Mulholland, 2004

The love we feel loving us is as much for those who wound and betray us, and for those we perceive as "enemies," as it is for ourselves. This love is for the lost and the broken; the cantankerous, ugly, and lonely; yes, and even the brutal, the murderous, and cruel. If we are to love God we must love them as well, not for their cruelties, but for the hidden Seed that would live and grow in them. We, who are loved with a love that will not let us go, are to let that same love flow through us into the world.

Carol Reilley Urner, 1994

We are asked to love as God loves,
showering sunshine and rain on the good and evil alike.
We are not told in the Sermon on the Mount
what the outcome of our actions will be.
But we may assume that closing off our love to an antagonist
carries no possibility of change in our relationship,
while continuing to love holds out the possibility of transformation. . . .
If we choose love, the peaceable commonwealth has already come
    to birth in our lives.
If we choose hatred or fear, the commonwealth is far away.

Sandra Cronk, 1984

"The job of the peacemaker is"
to know there is no enemy
what we fear are fear-masks
worn by ourselves
and "the other side,"
and behind each mask
• the hooded Klansman
• the complacent housewife
• the rich who seek more riches
Is something trembling
to be born:
something pure in eclipse
some love waiting to be released
a person deserving
reverence and faith.

Gene Knudsen Hoffman, 1995

While loving one's enemies does not necessarily mean liking them or even approving of them, it always means treating them as fellow human beings and not denying their humanity, as war always does. There is nothing in the life of Christ which says one cannot have opponents and even persecutors, but one cannot really have enemies, people whose lives and welfare have a negative value for you.

Kenneth E. Boulding, 1986

Projection occurs where one is dimly aware that they have a defect of character or a wrongful motive but is unwilling to acknowledge it even to themselves. This creates a conflict within them between their lower nature and their conscience. They have an underlying feeling of shame and a sense of guilt. In desperation they proceed to "project" the fault or harmful motive upon, or impute it to, some other person or group of persons. Then they can speak of it openly, blind themselves completely to its existence in themselves, and attack the other person for it. Thus by this self-deception they relieve their conflict and satisfy their conscience.

Richard B. Gregg, 1959

Our peacemaking cannot wait until we feel completely loving.
Feelings are notoriously unreliable guides.
We are called to obedient love
even though we may not be feeling very loving.
Often it is through the performance of loving acts
that loving feelings can be built up in us.
We may start with small, perhaps very tiny steps.

Sandra Cronk, 1984

. . . My tactic has been to stand in the face of [hate bred of fear and ignorance], smile lovingly at the person behind it, and simply hold it so others don't have to. Using this spiritual discipline of separating the hate from the person and working to love the person is a political tactic that helps keep me effective as a peace keeper, keeps me whole as a person, and creates hope.

Lisa Graustein, 2005

"Why do you come here? Why do you keep coming?" a soldier near Emerald Camp [asked] on an earlier visit. "It's no use, there's nothing you can do, what do you women think you can do by coming here? The missiles are here, you won't change anything, why do you come?"

[We answered] "We come to watch, we come to witness, we come with our hands full of ribbon and wool, flowers, and photos of loved ones, hands full of poems and statements and prayers, hands full of hope and knowledge that such hope is impossible to rational minds. . . . [We] come to talk with the police, the soldiers, men who might be gardeners standing by the tomb; [we] come to meet the Christ in them."

A member of the Quaker Women's Group vigiling against the cruise missile base at Greenham Common in 1986

Winning wars, in my lifetime, has never brought peace. Only after World War II, when we displayed love for our former enemies with the Marshall Plan and after Vietnam, when we gradually restored normal relations after withdrawing from the war, have we had peace after war.

Charles Brown, 2002

And you in that state, are to pray for the enemies that put you there; and if they curse and hate you, you are to bless them, and do good to them and you are to pray for them that despitefully use you, and persecute you, and love your enemies, that you may be children of your God which is in heaven.

George Fox, 1684

Our truth is an ancient one:
that love endures and overcomes;
that hatred destroys;
that what is obtained by love is retained,
but what is obtained by hatred proves a burden.

*Study of International Conflict, prepared for the American Friends
Service Committee, 1955*

Queries

When have I been able to transform my fear or dislike of someone who threatened me into some level of toleration, acceptance, or love? What made this possible?

When have I been aware of projecting my fears and anxieties on those who threaten me? What was the effect of this projection?

In what ways am I endeavoring to face the evil in the world and to match it with redemptive love?

Practicing Peace in the World
through Nonviolent Action

Not by might
nor by power,
but by my Spirit. . . .

Zechariah 4:6

In an effort to bring racial equality and stop violence during the 1960s, the National Council of Negro Women invited interracial, interfaith teams of northern women to participate in a project called "Wednesdays in Mississippi." Every Wednesday, teams of northern women visited freedom schools, watched voter registration, and quietly reached out to wives of Mississippi businessmen with tea parties and luncheons in an effort to build behind-the-scenes lines of communication.[7]

Some local people, however, resented the presence of these northern women, and responded with violence. One night Fay Honey Knopp, a Wednesdays in Mississippi team member from Connecticut, was driving a carload of black and white women along a lonely back road when a pickup truck began harassing them in a way that was clearly meant to be threatening. The tension in the car rose as the women became aware of the likelihood of serious violence. But Honey was determined to confront this threat nonviolently. She stopped the car in the middle of the road, rolled down her window, waved to the men in the truck in a friendly way, and called out warmly: "Are you lost? Can we help you?" The men, disconcerted and deflated by her open, friendly manner, hesitated for a few moments and then drove away.[8]

Honey's inspired response rose out of her nonviolence training and her willingness to rely on God's transforming power. Her proactive, nonviolent approach involved trusting the Spirit, recognizing the potential good in the aggressor, and reaching out in a creative, unexpected, and loving way. By engaging in nonviolence, Fay Honey Knopp not only kept herself safe, but she also restrained her would-be attackers from degrading themselves through an act of violence.

Of course, nonviolent action cannot always protect us from harm, any more than violence can. However, by choosing nonviolent means, we not only create new possibilities for reconciliation, but we also open pathways for God's spirit to leave its indelible mark of healing and love on the world.

. . . Nonviolent resistance acts as a sort of moral jiu-jitsu. The nonviolence and good will of the victim act in the same way that the lack of physical opposition by the user of physical jiu-jitsu does, causing the attacker to lose their moral balance. They suddenly and unexpectedly lose the moral support, which the usual violent resistance of most victims would render them. They plunge forward, as it were, into a new world of values. They feel insecure because of the novelty of the situation and their ignorance of how to handle it. They lose their poise and self-confidence. The victim not only lets the attacker come, but, as it were, pulls them forward by kindness, generosity and voluntary suffering, so that the attacker loses their moral balance.

Richard B. Gregg, 1959

At [age] 20 in the Arlington, Virginia, sit-ins in which black [and white] activists pressured shop owners to desegregate lunch counters by sitting peacefully in restaurant seats, [David Hartsough] was confronted by a switchblade-wielding white telling him that he had two seconds to leave. "I'll still try to love you, but do what you think is right," David told his attacker. The attacker's jaw dropped, then he left.

Chris Richards, 2004

Evil must be resisted, nonviolently but absolutely,
as much for the sake of the evildoer
as for the prevention of the wrong they attempt.
Those who do wrong are harming themselves and need saving,
rescuing if you like, from the evil that they practice or contemplate.
They are men and women who are capable of goodness;
and the method of nonviolence seeks to turn them from evildoing
to well-doing.

Kathleen Lonsdale, 1957

Perhaps most important and most often misunderstood, is that nonviolence is essentially confrontational. It is prepared to resist injustice and wrong whenever it occurs, fearlessly and honestly. In so doing, the nonviolent activist is often perceived as creating disorder, rocking the boat and stirring up trouble. . . .

This was particularly so in apartheid South Africa, where campaigners were often accused of stirring up trouble and violence, while what they were really doing was exposing the massive structural violence of a racist regime. Nonviolence exposes the latent violence of society, by lovingly confronting injustice. . . .

Helen Steven, 2005

Amanda Way, a nineteenth-century abolitionist and temperance reformer from Kansas was concerned about the large numbers of husbands and fathers who spent their family's food money at local saloons. While some women in the temperance movement were outraged by the plight of these hungry families and tried to close the saloons by using axes to tear up barrooms, Amanda consistently looked for nonviolent alternatives.

She knew that bars offered their patrons a free lunch, so she organized groups of poor families to go into the bars and eat the free lunches offered there. It is easy to imagine the surprise and consternation of the saloon owners when the hungry women and children arrived, sat at the bar, and ate all the food, making the point that fathers who drank regularly often took food away from their families.

Based on an interview with historian Margaret Hope Bacon

. . . When the United States was experiencing agriculture surpluses in the early 1950s, the American Friends Service Committee initiated a campaign to call attention to a terrible famine in China by mailing small sacks of potatoes with a note attached: "If thine enemy hungers, feed them" (Proverbs 25:21). At that time tensions were high over threatened attacks by the Mainland Chinese on islands in the straits of Formosa. President Dwight Eisenhower was meeting with the Joint Chiefs of Staff to decide whether or not to strike China with atomic bombs. The president sent an aide to find out how many sacks of potatoes had arrived, who returned to report that they had received 40,000. Dwight Eisenhower is reported to have said: "If 40,000 Americans think we should be feeding the Chinese, what are we doing thinking about bombing them?" As history silently records, the bombing did not happen.

John H. Darnell, 2003

Alternatives To Violence Guidelines

- Seek to resolve conflicts by reaching common ground.

- Reach for that something in others that seeks to do good for the self and for others.

- Listen. Everybody has made a journey. . . .

- Base your position on truth. . . .

- Be ready to revise your position if you discover it is not fair to all . . . do not expect that this response will automatically ward off danger. If you cannot avoid risk, risk being creative rather than violent.

- Surprise and humor can help transform violence into non-violence.

- Learn to trust your inner sense of when to act and when to withdraw.

- Be willing to suffer suspicion, hostility, rejection, and even persecution if necessary.

- Be patient and persistent in the continuing search for injustice.

- Help build a community based on honesty, respect, and caring.

- Build your own self-respect.

- Respect and care about others.

- Expect the best. . . .

- Pause and give yourself time before acting or reacting. . . .

- Trust your inner sense of what's needed. . . .

- When you have done wrong, admit it, make amends, and then let it go.

- Don't threaten or put down.

- Make friends who will support you. . . .

- Risk changing yourself.

Harold Wilson, 2002

[Thomas Garret was] hauled into court and so heavily fined for his activity in the underground railway that he was left financially ruined. Garrett stood before the Court and uttered these words, "Judge, thou hast left me not a dollar, but I wish to say to thee and to all in this courtroom that if any one knows a fugitive who wants a shelter and a friend, send him to Thomas Garrett and he will befriend him." . . .

Such defiance was regarded then, as it would be regarded today, as a foolish and impractical gesture, calculated only to have its perpetrator held in contempt. But humanity's judgment was in error then as we believe it to be in error today, for it neglected to calculate the impact of stirring example. It is precisely the demonstration of this kind of unlimited faith that shakes human souls, and when this happens, the impossible moves nearer to the possible.

Study of International Conflict, prepared for the American Friends Service Committee, 1955

When we are confronted with hurt to ourselves or others, and the rational ways of mending it are not effective, we are forced to choose between complicity in the universal wrong and an act of sacrifice. Then the divine voice inside us insists that this is the most important choice of all. . . .

The journey of renunciation, the heroism [which] may be called for within our own hearts, [is] a private matter between us and God. It happens when we accept the hurt, and do not let it enslave or degrade us, but endure it, and refuse to pass it on. When we choose this path, we cannot foresee its end; we can't say if it will do any good. It is a starting point, not a solution. We don't know what will be asked of us next. But by this sacrifice we have identified ourselves with whatever power there is in the universe to redeem and recreate. . . .

John Lampen, 1987

Whereas violence generally seeks the good of only one contending party, nonviolent direct action, guided by love, seeks the personal fulfillment of all concerned. It is practical in the sense that while one cannot be sure of the effects of specific acts, one can know that love is good and must eventually produce good fruit. . . .

Phillips P. Moulton, 1971

Early one Sunday morning, I went for a walk in the Old City of Jerusalem. A group of Israeli Soldiers near the Damascus Gate was stopping Palestinian men for ID checks. In consequence of listening to experienced members of the CPT (Christian Peace Team) in Hebron over the previous week, I knew enough to walk past the soldiers but stop and watch what was going on from about 20 yards away.

In succession, three young men were stopped. Two were released, but three soldiers continued questioning the third. Two additional soldiers came over and very soon, one of new soldiers raised his arm and slapped the man on the face. He was about to strike a second time when I advanced a few paces and said loudly, "Hey why are you doing that?"

The soldier lowered his arm and said something in Hebrew to me, to which I responded, "You don't need to do that." He and his buddy left the group and walked past me through the Gate. I continued to watch and one of the other soldiers said something to me in Hebrew, signaling with his arms that he wanted me to leave. But I continued to watch. In another minute or so, the soldiers released the man and the incident was over.

As we walked out through the Damascus Gate together, the Palestinian and I soon determined that he spoke no English and I no Arabic. At the top of the steps we parted with a handshake. What struck me was that he was somewhere in age between that of my two sons, age 17 and 20. I couldn't help thinking what emotional scars they would carry from an encounter like that. But this was a minor experience, common to life under occupation.

The soldiers, too, were of the same age. In the last week, six of their own were killed at a checkpoint north of Ramallah. No one should be in these positions, particularly children.

Ben Richmond, 2002

We come together because a young man, nearly two thousand years ago, took this road [of nonviolence]. We argue now about who he was, or how we should interpret the records of him. Whatever is obscure, we can see one thing clearly. . . . Jesus refused to let Peter fight. . . . He would not forge the next link in the chain of hurt and revenge. He allowed all those others to crush him with their pain and hate, unresisting, forgiving, trusting that he could take all their evil into himself and so bring it to an end.

John Lampen, 1987

A victory by nonviolence does not carry with it a further latent threat to harm anyone. It carries conviction of sincerity and friendship, whereas a victory through violence always has in it at least a suspicion of selfishness and possible further aggrandizement. In quality a victory by nonviolent resistance is far more gallant and joyous than one by violence can ever be. It requires no lying, distortion, or suppression of the truth, no slaughter or threats. it leaves no bad conscience or bad taste in the mouth. The public opinion it gains is weighty and lasting.

Richard B. Gregg, 1959

Effective nonviolent political action does not spring from a vacuum. It grows out of daily living grounded in personal and communal spiritual practice, and in constructive service to one's immediate and surrounding communities. Nonviolence on the political stage is only as powerful as the personal and community-based nonviolence of those who engage in it. . . .

No one can build an integrated nonviolent life as an individual. I may be able to practice some measure of piecemeal nonviolence more or less on my own. But if I'm going to pluck the seeds of war from each part of my life that I possibly can, if I am going to renounce and abandon the violence of my first-world way of life, I need to be surrounded by others whose knowledge, wisdom, and experience will complement mine, and whose example and company will inspire me to stay the course.

Chris Moore-Backman, 2006

We are not naïve or ignorant about the complexity of our modern world and the impact of sophisticated technologies—but we see no reason whatsoever to change or weaken our vision of the peace that everyone needs in order to survive and flourish on a healthy, abundant earth.

The primary reason for this stand is our conviction that there is that of God in every one which makes each person too precious to damage or destroy.

While someone lives, there is always the hope of reaching that of God within them: such hope motivates our search to find nonviolent resolution of conflict.

Peacemakers are also empowered by that of God in them. Our individual human skills, courage, endurance, and wisdom are vastly augmented by the power of the loving Spirit that connects all people.

Refusal to fight with weapons is not surrender. We are not passive when threatened by the greedy, the cruel, the tyrant, the unjust.

We will struggle to remove the causes of impasse and confrontation by every means of nonviolent resistance available.

There is no guarantee that our resistance will be any more successful or any less risky than military tactics. At least our means will be suited to our end.

If we seemed to fail finally, we would still rather suffer and die than inflict evil in order to save ourselves and what we hold dear.

If we succeed, there is no loser or winner, for the problem that led to conflict will have been resolved in a spirit of justice and tolerance. . . .

Conflicts are inevitable and must not be repressed or ignored but worked through painfully and carefully. We must develop the skills of being sensitive to oppression and grievances, sharing power in decision-making, creating consensus, and making reparation.

In speaking out, we acknowledge that we ourselves are as limited and as erring as anyone else. When put to the test, we each may fall short.

From the Yearly Meeting of the Religious Society of Friends
in New Zealand, 1987

Queries

What are examples from my own life—or from events I have observed—that represent nonviolent action? What have I learned from these experiences?

What do I see as the advantages of nonviolent action? What are my reservations about the use of active nonviolence in my personal life or as a strategy for social change?

What helps me accept and endure hurt without letting it degrade me and without passing it on?

What would help me be better prepared to participate in direct, nonviolent action?

Practicing Peace in the World
through Pacifism and Conscientious Objection

For though we live in the world
we are not carrying on a worldly war
for the weapons of our warfare are not worldly
but have divine power. . . .

2 Corinthians 10:3–4

As a Distinguished Graduate of the Air Force Academy, Charlie Clements had heard a lot about the Vietnam War long before he arrived in Southeast Asia. However, almost immediately he began to notice discrepancies between the official, public statements about the war and what he saw and experienced around him.[9]

Though Charlie had purposefully chosen a noncombatant role as a transport pilot, he began to realize that he was part of the machinery that made the war possible. After flying missions to the area from which the invasion of Cambodia would take place, Charlie decided that he would not fly any further combat missions. He was counseled by his commander that he was throwing away his career, but Charlie was adamant. He was examined by a flight surgeon and sent to the United States for evaluation. After a six-month stay in a psychiatric hospital he was honorably discharged with a 10 percent mental disability. Eventually, Charlie says, he figured out that the same piece of paper implied he was 90 percent intact, and with that he went to medical school.[10]

After becoming a Quaker and graduating from medical school, Charlie feared another Vietnam was unfolding in Central America. During the 1980s he volunteered to provide medical care to several thousand villagers in a rural province of El Salvador. American Friends Service Committee supervisor Stephen G. Cary once accompanied Charlie to a refugee camp outside San Salvador. Along the way, they passed a U.S. embassy car with darkened windows and armed escorts. Steve noted the contrast between the defensive secrecy of the officials and the reception Charlie received at the camp. He was immediately surrounded by a large crowd of laughing, shouting people, all trying to hug him at once.

That particular day, Charlie had brought a wheelchair for a five-year-old boy with polio. He gently placed the boy in the chair, then told him to put his hands on the wheels and push. When the child rolled a few feet forward, a look of awe spread over his face, and he burst into tears. It was the first time he had ever propelled himself. Charlie cried. Steve cried. Everyone in the crowd cried as "the little boy wheeled around the camp with about 100 children running after him."[11]

Steve later wrote: "I asked myself—my God, my God—what is the path to peace? Is it in those cars with their one-way glass and their shotgun escort, or is it in Charlie's wheelchair?"[12]

Pacifists believe that the way to peace lies not in waging war as the world does, but in following the path of love and compassion exemplified by Charlie Clement's wheelchair. Pacifism and conscientious objection are active, dynamic, and often risk-taking spiritual disciplines of living obedient to a God who challenges us to follow our conscience in acts of love and reconciliation.

We will not use weapons of war,
or willingly allow them to be used in our name.
We are called to resolve conflicts,
at whatever level, without violence.
We are prepared to pay the ultimate cost—
our lives if necessary—
to uphold this conviction,
which comes from our deepest roots,
that everyone has within them something of God which is sacred.
We can never deliberately destroy a person
without at the same time destroying a part of God.

Simon Fisher, 2004

It is a mistake to call Quakers "non-resisters" or "passivists." They are neither. They do not face any giant evil with a passive attitude. They seek always to organize and to level against it the most effective forces there are. They know as well as anybody does that instincts and passions are not changed by miracle and that peace cannot prevail where injustice and hate are rampant. They seek to do away with war by first doing away with the causes and occasions for it; that is, by removing the fundamental grounds from which war springs, by eliminating the roots and seeds of it in the social order, and by forming an atmosphere and climate that make war unthinkable.

Rufus M. Jones, 1927

Pacifism, which literally refers to
the making of peace (from *pace* and *facere*)
is often mistakenly understood as passivism.
One major attitudinal obstacle to the acceptance of peaceableness as a desirable social norm is
the connotation of inactivity associated with it.

Elise Boulding, 2000

Pacifism is not susceptible to easy understanding. . . . Each person must work out a definition of pacifism anew. At the same time, every pacifist has faced the same decisions. Varying in cultural details, these decisions answer the same question: Where does one's responsibility begin, and end? Can one stand watch for Spanish ships? Treat a wounded soldier? Spy on Indians? Designate the forts, when drawing up a map? Eat the king's food, while in the brig? Be a jailor? Redeem Quaker slaves from Morocco by selling arms?

Meredith Baldwin Weddle, 2001

By 1660 Quakers had decided that they could not serve in the army . . . perhaps as many as 15,000 Quakers were imprisoned, and 450 died. Their patient and persistent acceptance of suffering has often been cited as an antecedent to the modern practice of nonviolence. Their actions spoke to the conscience of many and led to the passage of the Toleration Act in 1689.

Margaret Hope Bacon, 1986

In 1861 a third-generation Quaker from Lake Champlain was drafted. "But it will be of no use," he said. "I shall never fight. My mother taught me it is a sin. It is her religion, and my father's, and their fathers.' I shall never raise my hand to kill anyone."

The recruiting officer took little notice. "We'll see about that later," he commented carelessly. . . . The lieutenant conferred with the captain, and all the forms of punishment devised for refractory soldiers were visited on him. He went through them without flinching, and there was only one thing left. He was taken before the colonel. "What does this mean?" demanded the officer. "Don't you know you will be shot?" "That is nothing," said the Quaker. "Thee didn't think I was afraid did thee?"

The colonel went to the President, to Lincoln. Lincoln listened and looked relieved. "Why, that is plain enough," he answered. "There is only one thing to do. Trump up some excuse and send him home. They can't kill a boy like that, you know. The country needs all her brave men wherever they are. Send him home."

Daniel Bassuk, 1987

Pacifism is not a tool or an instrument that you can pick up and lay down, use it today but not use it tomorrow, use it in one relationship of life but not in other relationships of life. It is, itself, a way of life that grows out of convictions, attitudes, and habits, which in time become an inseparable part of the pacifist individual.

A.J. Muste, 1941

Pacifists who have no inner sense of peace are not well fitted to work for peace. Their own inner conflict will infect what they do. Inner conflict as modern psychologists have often pointed out,

practicing peace   223 produces outer conflict, especially when that inner conflict is not recognized by those in whom it exists.

Howard Brinton, 1952

As I studied the Gospels, especially the Sermon on the Mount where Jesus tells us to love our enemies, it seemed clear to me that the New Testament said we must not kill. The early church of course had the same interpretation, and was pacifist until the time of Constantine. But, I did not know how to live that way. It seemed impractical.

At some point, I realized that my reluctance to accept what I saw as a clear teaching of the Gospel meant that I was saying I under-stood human nature and society better than Jesus. To reject the teaching about peace and loving our enemies was to say somehow that Jesus was naïve and I was smarter. Eventually, I came to accept the peace testimony on faith. In the years that followed, I have of course learned that God is quite practical and that Jesus understood human nature very well.

Mary Lord, 2005

In our view, to take life deliberately is to cease absolutely to love
    our neighbor
and to deny in ourselves the very quality that makes us human. . . .
Pacifists must be ready to die but not to kill. . . .
Willingness to die for a principle
is not the same thing as to kill for a cause.
Even when inspirited by the highest motives
the solider dies in an effort to destroy the enemy;
but Jesus raised no hand against those who destroyed his body.
The two types of sacrifice are different in kind.

Edgar B. Castle, 1961

To me, killing or preparation for killing is a definite contradiction to [feeling] love for my fellow human beings. I must ask myself the question, "To whom do I owe my highest loyalty?" . . . I feel that I owe my highest allegiance to the whole human race and to God. However, I feel that while my highest loyalty is to God and to the whole human race, it is at the same time the greatest loyalty I can give to my country.

*From David Hartsough's application to become
a conscientious objector, 1959*

The boy [Donald Groom] heard the letterbox rattle in the front door, heard a woman's footsteps move quickly down the front path and on to the street. He picked up the white feather that had fluttered onto the floor and attached itself to the fringe of the hallway mat. The child stood holding the feather in his cupped hands. He was only four years old, but he knew that the feather would mean more distress to his mother, more silent anger from his father. . . . The feathers were symbols of cowardice, usually handed out by women [in England], to shame men into active military service.

Victoria Rigney, 2002

I recall listening to Friend George Willoughby, still an active peacemaker in his mid-eighties, talking with a young Friend who said he might have chosen to join the army to fight against fascism in World War II. George, in a response which echoes Gandhi, said that he could understand why many people were led to join the military in the struggle to end fascist violence. But, he continued, he also fought fascism and violence. He just did it nonviolently. And he has continued to struggle nonviolently—and very creatively—for peace and justice his entire life. Gandhi himself said that the way of satyagraha—holding fast to truth, or what we generally call nonviolence—is only possible for very strong people. I believe we are called to be that strong people, or at least among a community of strong people, rejecting war and committed to nonviolent action for peace and justice.

Bruce Birchard, 2004

Mennonites, Brethren, and Friends developed CPT [Christian Peacemaker Teams] following a speech by Ron Sider at the

Mennonite World conference in 1984. He said: "Those who believed in peace through the sword have not hesitated to die. . . . Unless we . . . are ready to start to die by the thousands in dramatic vigorous new exploits for peace and justice, we should sadly confess that we never really meant what we said, and we dare never whisper another word about pacifism to our sisters and brothers in those desperate lands filled with injustice. Unless we are ready to die developing new nonviolent attempts to reduce conflict, we should confess that we never really meant that the cross was an alternative to the sword."

Ben Richmond, 2002

If I understand the message of God's response to that question [Why are we here in Iraq?] it is that we are to take part in the creation of the Peaceable Realm of God. Again, if I understand the message of God, how we take part in the creation of this realm is to love God with all our heart, our mind and our strength and to love our neighbors and enemies as we love God and ourselves.

Tom Fox, November 25, 2005, the day he and three other members of the Christian Peace Team in Baghdad, Iraq, were kidnapped. He was murdered almost four months later.

And even if one sees pacifist behavior as misguided, there is no mistaking the extraordinary physical courage pacifism sometimes requires.

Meredith Baldwin Weddle, 2001

Conscientious objection is. . . . refusal to surrender moral responsibility for one's action.

Kenneth C. Barnes, 1987

Our actions help create the future. . . . Every use of the sword multiplies future uses of the sword. Those that build their lives behind a sword-based defensive wall will stimulate in their neighbors and enemies symmetrical responses, as they equip themselves to deal with the new levels of threat in their lives. . . .

The pacifist realizes that [his or her] actions create the context for other actions. The costs of every act of killing include making the next act of killing more likely. Our society is stuck in the myth of effective violence, the notion that when you really mean business you do violence. So every act of violence adds weight to the myth.

Ron Mock, 2005

That which is set up by the sword,
is held up by the sword,
and that which is set up by spiritual weapons,
is held up by spiritual weapons,
and not by carnal weapons.
The peacemakers have the commonwealth, and are in it;
and hath the dominion over the peace-breaker,
to calm them in the power of God. . . .

George Fox, 1652

We [pacifists] knew our actions would not stop the war. . . .
What we did was to light a few candles in the darkness,
to keep the ideal of nonviolence alive
for use when the world came to its senses.

Larry Gara and Lenna Mae Gara, 1999

Queries

When have I refused to go along with something on the basis of conscience? What were the results or consequences of my refusal?

When have I gone along with something that violated my conscience? What were the results or consequences of my compliance?

How have I supported others in their decisions of conscience?

practicing peace

Practicing Peace in the World
through Accepting the Costs of Witnessing

I appeal to you therefore, brethren, by the mercies of God, to present your bodies as a living sacrifice, holy and acceptable to God. . . . Do not be conformed to this world but be transformed by the renewal of your mind, that you may prove what is the will of God, what is good and acceptable and perfect.

Romans 12:1–2

In 1832 Prudence Crandall was running a successful girls' school in Canterbury Green, Connecticut. But when she agreed to teach Sarah Harris, an African American girl who wanted to become a teacher, the parents of Prudence's European American students became enraged, and demanded that Sarah be expelled immediately. Instead, Prudence sent her European American students home and began a school for African American girls.

The community was furious. Locals filled her well with manure, refused to share their water, and finally jailed her for teaching African American girls to read and write. People from the community tried to burn her house down, and one night they surrounded her home when she and her students were inside and methodically beat in all the windows and doors. Prudence finally had to abandon her school and leave town, but her courage and the high cost of her witness were reported around the country and moved others to take stands against racial discrimination.[13]

In early Anglo Saxon, the word *bless* meant to make sacred by sacrifice.[14] Prudence blessed others by her willingness to risk sacrificing her safety, her career, and her school. We bless others when we sacrificially raise children, make lifestyle adjustments to preserve the environment, or risk alienation from our community by witnessing for an unpopular cause. Like Prudence Crandall, when we bestow blessings through sacrificial service we cannot know in advance what costs, emotional sufferings, social gains, or spiritual rewards may attend our witness.

"So this is what I want from you," I imagine Jesus saying.
"I want you to accept what happens to me as a fulfillment,
and not as an accident I should have tried to avoid.
And frankly, I expect nothing less from the rest of you.
I want you to remember that,
even as you pick up a loaf of bread and break it, and eat it,
you have in your hands a reminder of one of the principal truths
    of life:
if you deny yourself, each one of you,
and if you accept whatever pain may come to you because of me,
then you will really find yourself;
but if you try to avoid the pain and save yourselves from trouble,
I assure you, you will lose the whole purpose of living."

Gilbert L. Johnston, 1999

This choice [of whether to witness for God] is no less important when it takes place in secret, among the daily knocks and disappointments of what is called a humdrum life. It is easier for me to call those witnesses whose sacrifices took place on a public stage; but I am talking about something, which does not usually demand long journeys, dramatic renunciations, or heroic endurance, in the sense that the people around us will recognize. The journey, the renunciation, the heroism, may be called for within our own hearts, a private matter between us and God.

John Lampen, 1987

Some of us aren't called to the edge,
but our role is no less important.
In fact, if we aren't faithful to our piece,
those who are called to the edge cannot be faithful to go to the edge.

Deborah Fisch, 2003

There is no doubt that prophetic action is costly.
A Quaker Peace and Service poster says,
"Let us take the risks of peace upon ourselves
and not impose the risks of war on others."
Opposing the structures of power, oppression, and exploitation is
  dangerous.
It can mean loss of friends, job, status, health, even life itself.
But it is just such actions of visible risk-taking that move people
  to change.

Helen Steven, 2005

If I lived as if resurrection were real,
and allowed myself to die for the sake of new life,
what might I be called upon to do?
What strange and difficult tasks might be laid upon me,
what comforts taken away?

Parker J. Palmer, 1990

No pain, no palm,
no thorns, no throne,
no gall, no glory,
no cross, no crown.

William Penn, 1682

Mary Dyer was an English Quaker who was jailed by the Puritans
in 1657 under an ordinance that outlawed Quakers. Even though
she was banned from the Massachusetts Bay Colony she kept
going back, because she felt led by God to continue to preach her

truth. The result of her persistent witness was that she was one of four Quakers hanged on Boston Common in October of 1659, and the disgrace of her hanging was part of what eventually led England to allow religious freedom in the colonies. James Bowden wrote, "The ultimate prevalence of religious toleration in the western world (came about) through the constancy and faithfulness of Friends." . . .

Today, Mary Dyer's statue . . . stands [outside the Massachusetts state house], a symbol of the struggle for religious freedom. School children learn to recite her plea to the Boston court: "In love and meekness I beseech you to repeal these cruel laws to stay this wicked sentence. . . . But if one of us must die that others may live, let me be the one . . . for what is life compared to the witness of Truth?"

Based on information from George Selleck and
Margaret Hope Bacon, 1980

Be willing that self shall suffer for Truth
and not the Truth for self.

James Parnell, 1656

There is a parable told of a person arriving at the judgment seat, and being asked, "Where are your wounds?" When the supplicant admits to being unscathed and bearing no wounds, the question comes, "Was there nothing worth fighting for?"

Helen Steven, 2005

I can think of no more awful heresy
which has assailed the modern church
than the belief that
peace can be had on this earth without suffering for it—
suffering with the faith that
love will surely have the final word. . . .

James Kilpatrick, 1946

This is a very tight situation—no books from the outside, visitors list not yet approved on the 18th day, limitations on postage stamps. I'm trying to learn patience here. It is very noisy and smoky. We must all wear uniforms. Mine is too big for me, so I look like a clown. . . . [Yet] it feels good to be doing this [jail time for protesting the preparation for nuclear war] and the support has been incredible. I have been amazed at the response in my community to the idea of a 64-year old grandmother in jail. I think our short 30 days in here will really move others to look at what they might do that they are not doing, from vigiling to wiring letters to the editor to joining a peace groups . . . who knows. . . ?

Frances Crowe, 1984

What we're going through in our society
makes it a time when true believers have to step up to the plate.
We're going to have to speak as God would have us speak.
And when we do that it may not make us popular
with our congregations, with our community, with our family. . . .

Deborah Saunders, 2004

Better to run the possible risk of fanaticism by complete dedication to God than to run the certain risk of mediocrity by twenty percent dedication. . . . Concerning such, the Scriptures say, "They, measuring themselves, by themselves, are not wise." The Prophets come to the world and say, "Thus saith the Lord." They don't say, "Thus saith the majority."

Thomas R. Kelly, 1938

Now is the time to risk being unpopular, to risk being called names—cowards, yellow bellies, enemy sympathizers—and being dismissed as naïve and irrelevant. Now is the time to write and speak and act against this coming war, at the risk of getting our names on the suspect-lists of patriotic watchdog organizations.

Now is the time to update our dossiers in various government security agencies.

Rufus Jones said in 1919. . . . "Two hundred years from now they will not remember your names, they will not have a roll on which every name is listed. But this thing which you are doing will never cease, for when you translate Love into Life, when you become organs of God for a piece of service, nothing can obliterate it. . . ."

Paul A. Lacey, 2003

If there should be no spiritual volunteers in this crisis of human history to bear testimony to the truth and splendor of this brave way of life for which Christ lived and died, then the final victory of arms by the successful bombing of cities and sinking of fleets and destruction of armies can hardly save the faith of the ages. Somebody must love it enough and be enough educated to it to refuse to compromise or to count the cost, or to argue about what might happen if something else isn't done. When the price-less jewel of the soul is at issue, you do not argue or insist, or halt between two opinions. You say, "I cannot do otherwise. God help me. Amen."

Rufus M. Jones, 1916

. . . Undoubtedly a time of suffering lies ahead for those who take their stand with the God of Peace on behalf of the Commonwealth of God which calls for more courage, more divine and wholehearted devotion than any soldiering of humankind's creation. It is well to count the cost before the bat-tle joins. All people will certainly cease to speak well of us; trade relationships may be crippled; children may be disqualified from some auspicious career. On the other hand, if we give way before the storm and our witness perish, no doubt deliverance will still come to humanity in another way and from another place, but "who knoweth whether we are not come to the commonwealth for such a time as this?"

Joshua Rowntree, 1913

Full long our feet the flowery ways
Of peace have trod,
Content with creed and garb and phrase:

A harder path in earlier days
Led up to God. . . .

But now the cross our worthies bore
On us is laid.
Profession's quiet sleep is o'er,
And in the scale of truth once more
Our faith is weighed.

The leveled gun, the battle-brand
We may not take:
But calmly loyal we can stand
And suffer with our suffering land
For conscience' sake.

John Greenleaf Whittier, 1863

Queries

When have I given or received the blessings of personal sacrifice?

When have I stood by my spiritual values, even though they were unpopular?

Am I called to witness on the edge? If not, how do I support others who are doing so?

How is God currently calling me to witness in my personal or public life? Are there risks or costs that make me hesitant to respond to that call?

Practicing Peace in the World
through Patience and Endurance

Therefore, my beloved brethren, be steadfast,
immovable,
always abounding in the work of God,
knowing that in God your labor is not in vain.

1 Corinthians 15:58

In 1944 Margaret Hope Bacon stepped into a maelstrom of suffering when she accompanied her new husband, Allen, to his conscientious objector placement at a state mental hospital in Maryland. There Margaret witnessed unimaginable suffering and needed unremitting patience to endure the long, hazardous days she spent working with potentially violent patients. Tranquilizers were not available, and the building was dark, rank, and noisy. She described it as a place where "disturbed patients roamed about the halls, hallucinating and shouting, and often fighting."[15]

On her first day of work, Margaret was filled with fear when told to bathe Sophie Brown, the most uncontrollable woman on the unit. In addition to mental illness, Sophie suffered from tuberculosis of the bowels and Margaret found her huddled in a locked room, naked and mumbling. The stench was overwhelming. When Margaret greeted the woman, Sophie lunged at her, but Margaret was able to restrain her by pinning her arm to her back. When she held Sophie's bony, feverish body, Margaret felt her own fear subside as she was filled with a deep sense of compassion for Sophie's tragic condition. From that day on Margaret was genuinely fond of Sophie, and she was the only staff person with whom Sophie would cooperate.[16]

Eventually Margaret was transferred to another part of the hospital. Two years later she heard that Sophie experienced a short period of clarity and spoke coherently for the first time in twenty-two years as a result of a lobotomy. Some of her first words were, "How is that nice Mrs. Bacon? She is the only friend I've had since I came to this place."[17]

Sophie's inquiry confirmed Margaret Hope Bacon's belief that enduring patience, anchored in God's love, *can* break through isolation, comfort fears, and bring peace into the most difficult of circumstances. Having endured we can then gratefully acknowledge, as did the poet Emily Dickinson, "Lord, by thy favor thou has made my mountain to stand firm."[18]

This business of seeking the Commonwealth of God has been going on a long time. It's almost 3000 years since Isaiah wrote those beautiful words about beating swords into plowshares. . . . [M]ost of our work is like casting our bread upon the waters; we'll probably never know exactly what effect we had. And we don't need to know; we can leave that to God. Our business is to be faithful to God's will, not to plan out the world's future.

Susan Furry, 1981

Friends' work
depends not on the assurance of success,
but on the assurance that it is our duty so to act.

Henry Joel Cadbury, 1972

. . . I have learned a very significant lesson from the Jewish prophets.
. . . These prophets taught that God does not require us
to achieve any of the good tasks that humanity must pursue.
What God requires of us is that we not stop trying.

Bayard Rustin, 1987

. . . Patience obtains the victory,
runs the race,
and obtains the crown.

George Fox, 1664

One of the most painful lessons is that the work of peace and justice,
like the work of the Seed within,
is one of patient waiting.
Patience is an active condition of the spirit.
It can march; it can demonstrate; it can live in jails.
It can survive the long haul of transformation.

Douglas Gwyn, 1996

Once [Bayard Rustin, an African American civil right organizer]
went into a restaurant in Indianapolis and asked for a hamburger.
The woman said she couldn't serve him. "Why?" he asked. She
finally admitted that she was afraid she'd lose business. If people
saw him there, they wouldn't come in.

He suggested they try an experiment in extending democracy. He
would sit at a table near the door with a hamburger in front of
him but would not eat it. For ten minutes they would count the
number of people who left or did not come in because of him. If
there was one such person, he would leave. If not, he could eat
his hamburger.

Bayard waited for fifteen minutes. No one had left, and a couple
had come in, paying no attention to him. The woman brought
him a hot hamburger. "What would you like to drink?" she asked.

Marnie Clark, 2004

Blessed are those
that never give up the struggle
for the one living Truth.

Emilia Fogelklou, 1910

A local social worker at a shelter for homeless teens was concerned about a young man who wore a wool hat pulled down over his eyes, and whose pants often looked as if they were about to fall off. The scruffy young fellow walked with his head down and never made eye contact with anyone. The shelter worker decided that she would at least make a project of saying hello to this young man every time she saw him, even though he wasn't reciprocating.

For weeks there was little or no response to her greetings, and the fellow did not even look at her. Sometimes when she spoke to him he would spit, occasionally he would grunt a little, but usually he just looked the other way. Still she persisted in saying hello to him every day. Finally one morning he surprised her by saying: "I have been counting every time you said hello to me, and as of yesterday you had said hello to me thirty-two times. I decided that if you said hello to me one more time, that would be thirty-three greetings, and it would mean that I really am an okay human being. Today you said hello to me again, so I guess I must be okay." She was amazed, because she had no inkling that her greetings were having any affect at all. She never saw the young man again at the shelter.

Shared by Dorothy Grannell with Portland Friends Meeting, 2002

You will often feel discouraged in your service. . . . It is good not to think of one's faithfulness as depending upon "inspiration," in the common sense of that word. Typically, this implies a surge of energy and enthusiasm which makes things flow. There is adrenaline in it, and a sense of expanded possibilities. It does not last long; it is taxing on the body and the emotions, and soon runs out of steam, sapped by fatigue or opposition. . . . Be patient in seeking the place where you can feel [God], because it is in this presence that you can do the work of understanding and responding to your discouragement.

Brian Drayton, 2006

Strength is odd. Physically some people have it and some do not. It cannot be shared around. But spiritual strength can. . . . This may be the deepest mystical doctrine of the New Testament. It is telling us that when we feel weak, there is a power within us that will hold us up. It is Christ's power, but also the power of all his other disciples, because as Paul says, we are members one of another. We have spiritual strength in common and our spirituality gives us access to it. From this, among other things, come fortitude and endurance.

John Punshon, 1990

The extraordinary ordinariness of many of these [seventeenth-century Quaker] women . . . [is that] they went out into the streets, faced physical abuse and cried their message over baying opposition, then they went home to check the household accounts and feed and comfort their children.

Christine Trevett, 1991

Nor must we fear failure.
We remember that Christ's life
judged by the world's standards
was an absolute failure.
He died unresistingly,
the shameful death which crucifixion was,
a pacifist peasant who,
had he reached our shores today,
would very likely have been deported as an undesirable Asiatic alien.

A. Ruth Fry, 1951

No need to worry what to do. . . .
No need to feel that unless
we are demobilizing the armies or
stopping the arms races or dismantling the multinationals,
we are doing nothing.
We never know what ripples

spread from what seems the smallest action.
Only let us be led by the Spirit
and we will vanquish the philosophy of death.
This is the only preparation for peace.

Adam Curle, 1981

I am comforted by words sent by a friend, based on the Talmud:
"Do not be daunted by the enormity of the world's grief. Do
justly, now. Love mercy, now. Walk humbly, now. You are not
obligated to complete the work, but neither are you free to abandon it."

Charlie Clements, 2003

Our culture's fearful obsession with results has sometimes, ironi-
cally, led us to abandon great objectives and settle for trivial and
mediocre ends. The reason is simple. As long as "effectiveness" is
the ultimate standard by which we judge our actions, we will act
only toward ends we are sure we can achieve. People who undertake projects of real breadth and depth are very unlikely to be
"effective," since effectiveness is measured by short-term results
(never mind the fact that such people may be creating cultural
legacies by their "failures"). But people with small visions will win
the effectiveness awards, since those projects are so insignificant
that they can almost always "succeed."

Parker J. Palmer, 1990

Let go of the outcome of one's actions
in trust and confidence that they are not in vain,
that somewhere in the secret workings of God,
a change is taking place.
Because the evidence of history is that change *does* happen
—indeed, that is what history is.

Helen Steven, 2005

During a recent retreat's lively discussion about interdependence, a physician commented that the daunting complexity of our times often leaves him feeling overwhelmed and powerless. "If the world is so tangled, so much of a swamp, what can one person do that would possibly make any difference?" "That 's just the point," replied a young teacher. "If you really get interdependence in your bones, you realize that everything you do makes a difference. You *can't not* make a difference!" Then it's a matter of aligning ourselves with the forces that are making a positive difference. Paradoxically, it would seem, the very conditions that make us feel powerless can lead us through it.

Laurent A. Parks Daloz, 2004

So the Lord God of life and power keep you firm and constant every one . . . in everlasting love, with which God hath loved you, that you be not soon shaken in this time of tempest, but that upon the rock of ages you may stand rooted and grounded upon God, unmovable, whose faithfulness endures forever. . . .

Margaret Fell, 1658

Queries

When have I relied on God for the patience to endure a difficult time?

When I feel discouraged about the state of the world, what helps me keep going?

What helps me remember that although I am not obligated to complete the work of building the Commonwealth of God on Earth, neither am I free to abandon it?

Practicing Peace in the World through Hope

May the God of hope
fill you with all joy
and peace in believing,
so that by the power of the Holy Spirit
you may abound in hope.

Romans 15:13

South African barrister Albie Sachs, who eventually helped write the new South African constitution and became a Supreme Court justice, was repeatedly imprisoned during Apartheid for speaking out against racial discrimination. During one of his long sentences in solitary confinement, he grew despondent, became physically and emotionally exhausted, and began losing hope for both his personal survival and the moral endurance of his failing country. One day, in a desperate effort to break out of his isolation, he began to whistle Dvorak's "Going Home." To his amazement, a lilting whistled response came floating into his bleakest moment from a prisoner in the same cell block. It felt like a miracle. As they whistled bridges of Dvorak back and forth, his spirits were lifted by the melodious sharing, and his hopes for both his personal ability to carry on and for the survival of his country were restored. He did not know who was in the other cell, but he never stopped wondering who had restored his hope by whistling.[19]

Some years later while living in London in exile, he told this story during a public talk. Dorothy Adams, a black South African Quaker who was also in exile, approached him afterward and revealed herself as the unidentified whistler. Later, when Albie was nearly killed by a car-bomb and lost an arm, Dorothy agreed to work as his assistant. And after Nelson Mandela was released in 1990, they both returned to South Africa.[20]

We are all rescued again and again from despair by the ephemeral songs of hope that rise from the shards of our shattered dreams and broken hearts. But sometimes when the din of our grief and suffering overpowers these melodies, God sends us hope through the singing of others. And while we may feel that we are whistling our songs of hope into an empty void, we cannot know what healing power they may be bringing to others. Although our songs of hope may appear to be fragile messengers, over the centuries they have proved strong enough to soothe fears, calm anxieties, outlast hatreds, remove oppressors around the world, and provide the foundation upon which the Commonwealth of God on Earth is built.

In such a world as ours today,
no light glib word of hope dare be spoken. . . .
Only if we look long and deeply into the abyss of despair
do we dare to speak of hope. . . .
We dare not tell people to hope in God. . . .
unless we know what it means to have absolutely no other hope
    but in God.
But as we know something of such a profound and amazing assurance,
clear at the depths of our beings,
then we dare to proclaim it boldly in the midst of a world aflame.

Thomas R. Kelly, 1940

Are there any grounds for hope? George Fox, struggling with his own despair, spoke of coming into the "covenant of peace, which was before wars and strifes were." That which was before wars and strifes—that was the love, which begot creation. We must never forget that "love was the first motion." Every human being that comes into the world is capable of that love, but how to give expression to that love has to be learned. . . . The grounds for hope lie in recovering our understanding of the human capacity for love, coupled with the realization we cannot take it for granted. That capacity needs to be nurtured.

Elise Boulding, 2000

Martin Luther King [Jr.] said once in a sermon in Detroit that hope is not like wishful thinking. It is not daydreaming about nice things, that one wishes could happen. Nor is hope like optimism, a tendency to believe that things just have to turn out right. Hope, he said, is based on a reality. His hope, he said, was based on the reality of a loving God, and a "universe which bends toward justice" in the long run. He hoped because he believed in the reality of that loving God.

Ron Mock, 1997

Hold fast the hope
which anchors the soul,
which is sure and steadfast,
that you may float above the world's sea.
For your anchor holds sure and steadfast in the bottom,
let the winds, storms and raging waves rise never so high.
And your Star is fixed,
by which you may steer
to the eternal land of rest and Commonwealth of God.

George Fox, 1676

. . . The Promise has been spoken,
And God's word shall not be broken,
The time will come when "Nations shall learn war no more."

The day of peace is breaking,
The nations are awaking,
And war, the fell destroyer, shall lay waste the
earth no more;
The friends of peace have spoken,
The swords shall all be broken,
And songs of love fraternal drown the
cannons' roar.

C.Z. Whipple, 1872

I remember the words of an old Frenchman
that are said to have been spoken at Verdun
after almost countless months of agony and frustration:
"There are no hopeless situations.
There are only men and women who have grown hopeless about
   them."

Douglas Steere, 1982

I see this "end time" as a time for ending old ways of being and acting.
As a time for ending old fears that there's not enough to go around,
a time for replacing competition with cooperation,
a time for choosing simpler ways of living, a time for giving
   instead of getting,
a time for keeping our hearts open to new truths
which can lead us out of the nightmare reality.
I see this time as our opportunity to explore
and experiment with this law of spiritual change in our own lives,
beginning with little ways, infinitesimal ways,
which will lead us to the larger, broader ones. . . .
There are infinite possibilities for us, for our nation, for our world.

Gene Knudsen Hoffman, 1982

Usually, as we know, the evolution of plants and animals is made
by very slow, minute steps; one form scarcely varying from the
previous one. But on rare occasions Nature takes a real leap for-
wards. For instance, botanists have found that certain flowers,
including the Toad Flax have two completely different forms, the
variation from the normal being known as the Poloic form. No
intermediate forms are found, and in fact the change could not be
made step-by-step, as the whole structure of the flower is different, and intermediate forms would not enable the flower to fulfill
its functions. It is apparently a jump in Nature's processes from
one system to another, and it is such a jump, curtailing the slow
process of evolution, which I believe the world is urgently needing now. For this is a moment in the history of humankind when

great decisions and alterations must be made or a terrible catastrophe may occur.

A. Ruth Fry, 1949

According to [George Ellis], kenosis is a force permanently embedded in the universe and capable of inspiring humanity to reach ever higher. He gave an example of his theory: "In the history of our country [South Africa], there was very good reason to give up hope for the future. But in fact, the right thing to do was to hope it would come right. And hoping it would come right was already part of the force that helps to transform."

*Glenn Reinhart, writing about George Ellis, the South African
Quaker mathematician and cosmologist, and the
Templeton Prize winner's theory of kenosis, 2005*

Many times I have found
my way home in the dark
because my feet felt the road
when my eyes could not see it.
There is Something in us,
deeper than hands or feet,
that finds the way to the Central Reality,
and when we arrive we know it.

Rufus M. Jones, 1944

Have you ever seen a miracle? I have. Have you ever seen the water of ordinary human nature changed into the wine of divine creative living? I have. Have you ever seen men and women whose outer world was repellent, or tragic, or barren, or hopeless, yet who walked serene, triumphant, radiant, released, undismayed, living constructively, as if they were already in Eternity, and drew not their encouragement from time? I have. We all have. Such persons have meat to eat that the world knows not of. Their secret of life is not outside of them, or around them, it is within them. In a rocky land, they have a well of water springing up within them unto Eternal Life. Are you such a miracle of radiant eternity lived in the midst of time? Am I such a miracle? Are we people whose lives cannot be explained by our environment, but only by saying, The Eternal Life and Love are breaking through into time, at these points?

Thomas R. Kelly, 1940

I believe with all my heart that
every act, every word, every attitude and longing
that is creative is caught up in the heart of the Eternal and is
preserved. . . .
What each one of us does is more important than it would appear,
and hope can "spring eternal,"
for its triumph,
if we are in the hands of God,
is ultimate.

Dorothy Steere, 1955

I saw also that there was an ocean of darkness and death,
but an infinite ocean of light and love,
which flowed over the ocean of darkness:
and in that I saw the infinite love of God;
and I had great openings.

George Fox, 1647

Queries

When in my life have I "whistled" a song of hope for others? When have others "whistled" a song of hope for me?

Where do I turn to find hope for the future during this difficult time in history?

In what ways is my life a beacon of hope to others?

What are the activities I am involved in that are helping to create a more peaceful and hopeful world?

Acknowledgments

Appendix: Biographical Information on the Primary Authors

Notes

Glossary of Common Quaker Terms

Acknowledgments

Grateful acknowledgment is made to all those who shared their work. Every effort has been made to give proper acknowledgment to authors and copyright holders of the text herein. If any omissions or errors have been made, please notify the publisher, who will correct it in future editions. The following acknowledgments of excerpts of over 250 words or poetry are reprinted by permission.

Excerpts on pages 37, 139, 192 from *Whirlwind of Life: The Story of Emilia Fogelklou* by Malin Bergman Andrews, 2004, Quaker Books.

Excerpts on pages 114–115 by Kirsten Backstrom from *God the Trickster: A Perfect Paradox* by Ben Pink Dandelion, 2001, Quaker Books.

Excerpts on pages 168, 180, 187 from *Let This Life Speak: The Legacy of Henry Joel Cadbury* by Margaret Hope Bacon, 1987, University of Pennsylvania Press.

Excerpts on pages 49, 164–165, 172, 225 from *The Roots and Fruits of the Powerful Peace Testimony* by Bruce Birchard, 2004, Quaker Press of FGC.

Excerpts on pages 179–180 from *Sensing the Enemy* by Lady Borton, 1984, Doubleday.

Excerpts on pages 201, 222 from *Cultures of Peace: The Hidden Side of History* by Elise Boulding, 2000, Syracuse University Press.

Excerpts on pages 27, 30, 80 from *One Small Plot of Heaven* by Elise Boulding, 1989, Pendle Hill Publications.

Excerpts on pages 159, 163, 193–194, 209, 214–215 from *Speak Truth to Power: A Quaker Search for an Alternative to Violence* by Steven G. Cary, Chairman, 1955, American Friends Service Committee.

Excerpts on pages 62, 72–73, 90, 153, 192, 220–221 from *The Intrepid Quaker: One Man's Quest for Peace* by Steven G. Cary, 2003, Pendle Hill Publications.

Excerpts on pages 89–90, 107, 123 from *Faith in Action: Quaker Social Testimonies* edited by Elizabeth Cave and Ros Morley, 2000, Quaker Home Service.

Excerpts on pages 104 (Small), 104 (Swennerfelt), 104–105 (Darby), 105 (Swennerfelt) from *Earthcare for Friends* edited by Louis Cox, Ingrid Fabianson, Sandra Moon Farley, and Ruah Swennerfelt, 2004, Friends Committee on Unity with Nature.

Excerpts on pages 82, 132, 180, 202, 206, 207 from *Peace Be With You: A Study of the Spiritual Basis of the Friends Peace Testimony* by Sandra Cronk, 1984, The Tract Association of Friends.

Excerpts on pages 35, 48, 144, 148, 202–203, 239–240 from *True Justice: Quaker Peace Makers and Peace Making* by Adam Curle, 1981, Quaker Home Service.

Excerpts on pages 48, 97, 238 from *On Living with a Concern for Gospel Ministry* by Brian Drayton, 2006, Quaker Press of FGC.

Excerpts on pages 63, 70, 110, 124, 160, 164, 202 from *The World in My Heart* by Jo Farrow, 1990, Quaker Books.

Excerpts on pages 119, 221 from *Spirited Living: Waging Conflict, Building Peace* by Simon Fisher, Swarthmore Lecture 2004, Quaker Books.

Excerpts on pages 178, 190, 207, 211, 217 from *The Power of Nonviolence* by Richard B. Gregg, 1959, Fellowship Publications.

Excerpts on pages 69, 70, 90, 91, 146, 205 from *If God is Love* by Phillip Gulley and James Mulholland, 2004, Harpercollins.

Excerpts on pages 41–42 from "What Will You Meet in the Wilderness?" by Janet Hoffman, *Quaker Life*, November 2001.

Excerpts on pages 35 (Calvi), 36 (Wood), 46–47 (Fisher) from *Visioning and Empowering: Friends Peace Witness in a Time of Crisis* edited by Nancy Irving, Vicki Hain Poorman, and Margaret Fraiser, 2005 Friends World Committee for Consultation, Section of the Americas.

Excerpts on pages 65, 94–95, 133 from *Testament of Devotion* by Thomas R. Kelly, 1941, Harper and Row Publishers, Renewed 1969 by Lois Lael Kelly Stabler. New introduction copyright 1991 by HarperCollins Publishers, Reprinted by permission of HarperCollins Publishers.

Excerpts on pages 48, 232, 243, 246–247 from *The Eternal Promise* by Thomas R. Kelly edited by Richard M. Kelly, 1966, published by Harper & Row and reprinted by permission of Richard M. Kelly.

Excerpts on pages 215, 216–217, 229 from *Mending Hurts* by John Lampen, 1987, Quaker Home Service.

Excerpts on pages 62, 79, 98, 117, 192, 212 from *The Christian Life Lived Experimentally* by Kathleen Lonsdale, 1976, Quaker Home Service.

Excerpts on pages 42, 69, 95, 101, 158 from *Rhythms of the Inner Life: Yearning for Closeness with God* by Howard R. Macy, 1988, Chariot Victor Publishing.

Excerpts on pages 62, 71–72, 108, 129, 157, 171, 206 from *Compassionate Listening and Other Writings by Gene Knudsen Hoffman*, edited by Anthony Manousos, 2003 by Friends Bulletin.

Excerpts on page 7 from *Friends and Violence* by Marjorie Nelson, Quaker Press of the FGC.

Excerpts on pages 218–219 from a peace statement by New Zealand Quakers written at their Yearly Meeting in January, 1987.

Excerpts on page 159 from "Trauma Healing in Rwanda" by Adrien Niyongabo, *The Friend*, London, June 13, 2003.

Excerpts on pages 49, 71, 111, 116, 117, 185 from *The Works of Inazo Nitobe, Volumes 1 and 5*, 1938, University of Tokyo.

Excerpts on pages 82–83, 153, 172 from *Unlocking Horns: Forgiveness and Reconciliation in Burundi* by David Niyonzima and Lon Fendall, 2001, Barclay Press.

Excerpts on pages 56 (Haines), 109 (Irie), 151 (Clark-Halkin Imani), 190 (Pym), 205–206 (Urner) from *Faith and Practice of Philadelphia Yearly Meeting of the Religious Society of Friends*, Philadelphia Yearly Meeting of the Religious Society of Friends, 2002.

Excerpts on pages 215–216, 225–226 from "Valiant for Truth" by Ben Richmond, *Quaker Life*, May 2002.

Excerpts on pages 46, 55, 56, 146, 175, 212, 230, 231, 240 from *No Extraordinary Power: Prayer, Stillness and Activism* by Helen Steven, Swarthmore Lecture 2005, Quaker Books.

Excerpts on pages 57–58, 71, 88, 96–97, 200 from *Wrestling with Our Faith Tradition* by Lloyd Lee Wilson, 2005, Quaker Press of FGC.

Excerpts from the following *Friends Journal* magazines are reprinted by permission: Charles Brown, "Letter to the Editor," June 2002; Paul Buckley, "Enemies," December 2001; Henry Joel Cadbury, "Belief into Action, Action into Belief," February 15, 1985; Dee Birch Cameron, "Why Quakers Should Learn to Apologize," February 2003; Steven G. Cary, "A Response to September Eleventh," March 2002; Charlie Clements, "Collateral Damage," April 2003; Susan Corson-Finnerty, "Prepare for the Best," January 2000; Mary Ann Downey, "Prayers and Protests," February 2003; Brian Drayton, "Douglas Steere: The Mystical in the Everyday," March 2004; Brian Drayton, "James Nayler: The Lessons of Discernment," December 2003; Susan Furry, "The Peaceable Kingdom Is at Hand, August 1–15, 1981; Tom Gates, "Euthasasia and Assisted Suicide: A Faith Perspective," June 1998; Julie Gochenour, "Cold Spell," January 2003; Kat Griffith, "The Kingdom of the Committee and the Garbage Dump of God," March 2005; Cathy Habschmidt, "No Easy Answers," November 2004; Anne C. Highland, "Becoming an Instrument of Peace," May 2005; Gilbert L. Johnson, "Do This in Remembrance of Me," 1999; Chris Moor-Backman, "Walking with Gandhi," April 2006; Kara Newell, "Quaker Profiles: Bob Philbrook," July 2001; Lyman Randall, "Paradox, Key to Unlocking the Perfection Trap," September 1999; Amy Y. Robinson, "Where the Light Shines Through," June 2005; Julie Shaul, "Leadings, Leanings, and Other Voices," January 1999; Dorothy Steere, "The Substance of Hope," December 31, 1955; William Taber, "Friends: An Elite Group or a People to be Gathered?", January 2003; Elizabeth Watson, "Only the Wounded Can Heal,"

July 1–15, 1976; Lloyd Lee Wilson, "A Statement of Christian Pacifism," December 2003; Harold Wilson, "Transformation of Violence," October 2002; David Yount, "Reflections of a Convinced Friend," January 2003.

Excerpts from the following Friends United Press books are reprinted by permission: *Walk Worthy of Your Calling* edited by Margery Post Abbot and Peggy Senger Parsons; *The Faith and Practice of the Quakers* by Rufus M. Jones; *A Procession of Friends* by Daisy Newman; *Where Two or Three are Gathered, Someone Spills the Milk* by Tom Mullen.

Excerpts from the following Pendle Hill pamphlets are reprinted by permission: Margaret Hope Bacon, "Lucretia Mott Speaking: Excerpts from the Sermons and Speeches of a Famous Nineteenth Century Quaker Minister and Reformer"; Daniel Bassuk, "Abraham Lincoln and the Quakers"; Bruce Birchard, "The Burning One-ness Binding Everything: A Spiritual Journey"; Kenneth E. Boulding, "Mending Hurts"; Kenneth E. Boulding, "There is a Spirit: The Naylor Sonnets"; Ann Curo, "Meditation on the Prayer of St. Francis"; Emil Fuchs, "Christ in Catastrophe"; Tom Gates, "Sickness, Suffering, and Healing: More Stores from Another Place"; Elizabeth Janet Gray, "Anthology with Comments"; Felicity Kelcourse and J. Bill Ratliff, "Discernment: The Soul's Eye View"; Paul A. Lacy, "Leading and Being Led"; Keith R. Maddock, "Living Truth: A Spiritual Portrait of Pierre Ceresole"; Phillips P. Moulton, "Violence or Aggressive Nonviolent Resistance?"; A.J. Muste, "War is the Enemy"; Parker Palmer, "A Place Called Community"; George Peck, "Simplicity: A Rich Quaker's View"; Mary Kay Rehard, "Bringing God Home: Exploring Family Spirituality"; Douglas Steere, "The Hardest Journey"; Elisabeth Ostrander Sutton, "Treasure in Clay Jars"; Frances Irene Taber, "Come Inside and Rest a While"; Carol Reilly Urner, "The Kingdom and the Way"; Dan Wilson, "The Promise of Deliverance"; John Yungblut, "On Hallowing One's Diminishments."

Excerpts from the following Pendle Hill books and papers are reprinted by permission of Pendle Hill Publishing: *A Certain Kind of Perfection* by Margery Post Abbot; *Friends for Three Hundred Years* by Howard Brinton; *Reflections on Peace* by Adam Curle and Elise Boulding; *Nudged by the Spirit* by Charlotte Lyman Fardelmann; *Anthology With Comments* by Elizabeth Janet Grey; *The Pendle Hill Reader* edited by Harrymon Maurer; *Sustaining Peace Witness in the Twenty-First Century: Tapping the Peacemaking Potential of Evangelical Friends* by Ron Mock; *The World in Tune* by Elizabeth Gray Vining; *Quaker Reader* edited by J. West.

Excerpts from the following Quaker Books are reprinted by permission: *Broken for Life* by S. Joycelyn Burnell; *On Having a Sense of All Conditions* by Charles Carter; *Testimony and Tradition* by John Pushon; *Faithful Deeds: A Rough Guide to the Quaker Peace Testimony* by Quaker Peace and Social Witness;

No Extraordinary Power: Prayer, Stillness, and Activism by Helen Steven; *Affirming the Light: Ten Stories of Quaker Peace Witness* by editorial group Stuart Ullathorne, Janet Bloomfiled, Helen Bradford, and David Gee.

Excerpts from the following Quaker Home Service books are reprinted by permission of Quaker Home Service Publishing: *Broken for Life* by S. Joycelyn Burnell; *Approach to Quakerism* by Edgar B. Castle; *Faith in Action: Quaker Social Testimonies* by Elizabeth Cave and Ros Morley; *True Justice: Quaker Peace Makers and Quaker Peace Making* by Adam Curle; *The World in My Heart* by Jo Farrow; *The Amazing Fact of Quaker Worship* by George H. Gorman; *Facing Death* by Diane Lampen; *Mending Hurts* by John Lampen; *The Discovery of Quakerism* by Harold Loukes; *Forgiving Justice: A Quaker Vision for Criminal Justice* by Tim Newell; *Truth a Path and Not a Possession* by Damaris Parker-Rhodes; *The Way Out is the Way In* by Damaris Parker-Rhodes.

Excerpts from the following *Quaker Life* magazines are reprinted by permission: John H. Darnell, "A Report From a Parallel Universe," June 2003; Trish Edwards-Konic, "Valiant for the Truth," June 2003; Ramon Gonzalez Longoria Escalon, "Valiant for the Truth," October 2005; Pam Ferguson, "The Call to Forgiveness and Restoration," April 2005; Susan Furry, "Safe Thus Far," August 1980; Janet Hoffman, "The Surprise of Pentecost: One Spirit, Many Voices," October 2002; Jay Marshall, "I Am Not Healed Yet!", November 1998; Howard R. Macy, "Maybe God's Laughing," May 2003; Glen Reinhart, "Quakers in the News," November 2005; Ben Richmond, "Valiant for the Truth," May 2002; Brad Tricola, "Snow and the Rested Souls," January/February 2005; Miriam Khamadi Were, "A Call to Quakers for Stepped Up Evangelism," July 2002.

Many of the sources included here are from the Haverford College Quaker Collection, Haverford College, Haverford, Pennsylvania; the Friends Historical Library at Swarthmore College, Swarthmore, Pennsylvania; and the Swarthmore College Peace Collection, Swarthmore, Pennsylvania.

practicing peace

Biographical Information on the Primary Authors

Margaret Hope Bacon (1921–) Historian and author of numerous articles, short stories for national magazines, and books on Quaker history; she has also worked with AFSC.

Emily Greene Balch (1867–1961) Educator, social reformer, professor of economics and sociology at Wellesley College; national president and international honorary president of the Women's International Peace and Freedom League; co-recipient of the Nobel Peace Prize in 1946.

Hugh Barbour (1921–) Historian and author. Born in China to English missionary parents, was a Professor of Quaker History at Earlham College of Religion from 1953 to 1991.

Bruce Birchard (1945–) Peace worker in disarmament and peace conversion for the Peace Committee of Philadelphia Yearly Meeting; national coordinator of the Disarmament Program of the AFSC; General Secretary of Friends General Conference.

Elise Boulding (1920-) Sociologist and feminist with a commitment to peace studies and peace activism, Professor Emerita of Dartmouth College, and author of books on families, women's "herstory," and peace. She has received more than nineteen awards for peace, and was nominated for a Nobel Peace Prize.

Kenneth E. Boulding (1910–1993) Professor of Economics at universities on three continents and author of more than thirty books. He was a peace activist, who, along with his wife, Elise, helped establish peace studies as a discipline in the United States.

Howard Brinton (1884–1973) College professor; author. He was an AFSC worker in Germany and Poland and, with his wife Anna, was co-director of Pendle Hill Retreat Center.

Judy Brutz (1940–) Pastor, author, poet, pastoral counselor, and researcher and writer in the area of sexual abuse.

John Calvi (1952–) is a Quaker healer with a travelling ministry since 1982. www.johncalvi.com.

Henry Joel Cadbury (1883–1974) Biblical scholar, professor at Haverford and Harvard Colleges, and peace and civil rights activist. He provided leadership for twenty-four years for the AFSC, on whose behalf he accepted the Nobel Peace Prize in 1947 in a tuxedo he borrowed from the donated clothing room at Friends Meeting at Cambridge.

Stephen G. Cary (1915–2002) Administered and/or counseled American Friends Service Committee for more than fifty years on projects including relief efforts in post-war Europe, Civil Rights in the United States, and outreach in Southeast Asia. He later became an administrator at Haverford College.

Edgar B. Castle (1898–1973) British educator. He broadened curriculums and urged students to think for themselves while headmaster at Leighton Park and later as Professor of Education at Hull, England.

Sandra Cronk (1942–2000) Educator, author, and spiritual guide. She was one of the founders of The School of the Spirit.

Adam Curle (1916–) English educator, author, and mediator. He became sensitized to peace issues through his work in South Africa, established the Center for Studies in Education and Development at Harvard University, and was involved in international mediations including India and Pakistan, the Nigerian Government and Biafra, and various groups in Ireland.

Laurent A. Parks Daloz (1940–) Peace Corps volunteer in Nepal; educator, author, and environmental activist. He has been an educational consultant and college professor, and is currently working with the Leadership for the New Commons at the Whidbey Institute in Washington State.

Brian Drayton (1953–) Biologist, educator, author, and recorded minister in New England Yearly Meeting. He is especially concerned with peace and ministry among Friends.

Jo Farrow (1930–) Author and former General Secretary of Quaker Home Service in Britain. She is a member of the Quaker Women's Group.

Margaret Fell (1614–1702) English Friend often credited with the pivotal organizational development of the early Friends movement. She traveled widely in the ministry, suffered three imprisonments by the authorities, and authored many tracts, including *Women's Speaking Justified*, the first justification written by a woman in defense of women's right to participate fully in all aspects of religious life. She later married George Fox.

Lon Fendall (1941–) Director for the Center for Global Studies and Center for Peace and Justice at George Fox University, author, and chair of the advisory committee of the Great Lakes School of Theology in Burundi.

Deborah Fisch (1959–) Editor, writer, and coordinator of the Traveling Ministries program for Friends General Conference.

Simon Fisher (1948–) British peace activist. He is a founder and co-director of Responding to Conflict, a world-wide peacemaking program.

Emilia Fogelklou (1878–1972) Educator, author, and mystic who worked on behalf of peace and women's concerns. She was the first woman in Sweden to earn a doctorate in theology.

Richard J. Foster (1942–) Writer, teacher, author, theologian, and founder of RENOVARE, an intrachurch movement committed to the renewal of the Church in all her multifaceted expressions.

George Fox (1624–1691) English spiritual seeker whose religious awakening resulted in the formation of the Religious Society of Friends. He travelled widely in the ministry, was married to Margaret Fell, and wrote prolifically, despite religious persecution and frequent imprisonment by the authorities.

Susan Furry (1944–) Her concern for ministry and peace has been expressed in work with AFSC, FUM, and FWCC, development of the Puente de Amigos between New England and Cuba yearly meetings, and war tax resistance.

A. Ruth Fry (1905–1962) English Friend, author, speaker, and international peace activist. She was General Secretary of both the Friends Relief Commission and the Russian Famine Relief.

Richard B. Greg (1885–1974) Writer, author, and attorney who worked in industrial relations. He was peace activist who became a personal friend to Mahatma Gandhi and who lived for a period at Gandhi's ashram.

Phillip Gulley (1961–) Pastor, theologian, and novelist. He is involved in a wide variety of community and social concerns.

Douglas Gwyn (1948–) Pastor, author, teacher, scholar in residence at Pendle Hill Retreat Center, and member of the staff of Woodbrooke in England.

David Hartsough (1940–) Peace activist with AFSC and Peace Brigades International; and cofounder of the Nonviolent Peaceforce, which is building a trained, international civilian peace force to go into conflicted areas in an effort to prevent death and protect human rights.

Janet Hoffman (1939–) A primary focus on faithfulness to God's voice has led her to speak and lead workshops in North America and abroad on Quaker ways of personal and corporate discernment, the liberating power of spiritual disciplines, and particular messages to be offered to specific faith communities.

Rufus Jones (1863–1948) Mystic, professor of philosophy at Haverford College, author of fifty-four books, international lecturer. In 1938 he attempted to negotiate freedom for the Jews by traveling to Nazi Germany with a small group of Friends where they met with leaders of the Nazi Secret Service.

Vanessa Julye (1960–) Educator, workshop leader, and author focusing on eradicating and healing the wounds of racism both within the Society of Friends and in society at large.

Thomas R. Kelly (1893–1941) Mystic, professor of philosophy at Haverford College, and author of a contemplative classic (*A Testament of Devotion*). He lived with deep compassion and a sense of the unity of humankind.

Bill Kreidler (1953–2000) Teacher, peace educator, and author of violence prevention curriculums. He lectured and developed materials for Educators for Social Responsibility.

Gene Knudson Hoffman (1919–) Social activist, author, and founder of the Compassionate Listening Project.

Ham Sok-Hon (1901–1989) Liberation theologian, farmer, author, and prisoner. He is respected in East Asia as the "Gandhi of Korea."

Paul A. Lacey (1934–) Author and professor of literature at Earlham College. He is active in civil rights, civil liberties, peace, and the American Friends Service Committee.

Diana Lampen (1940–) and John Lampen (1938-) British Friends who ran a school for emotionally disturbed boys for twenty years, lived and worked in Northern Ireland in the middle of violent conflict, and are now teaching peacemaking, relaxation, and meditation to groups in many parts of the world.

Kathleen Lonsdale (1903–1971) First woman to become a Fellow of the Royal Society; first woman President of the British Association for the Advancement of Science; prolific writer and peace advocate. She served a term of imprisonment during the war as a conscientious objector.

Mary Lord (1945–) Administrator and educator with the Physicians for Social Responsibility, Friends Committee on Legislation, and the American Friends Service Committee.

Howard R. Macy (1944–) Professor of Religion and Biblical Studies at George Fox University, writer, and author. He is involved in youth work, pastoring, and retreat leadership.

Ron Mock (1956–) Attorney and mediator; Professor of Political Science and Peace Studies at George Fox University; member of the International Quaker Working Party on Israel and Palestine.

Lucretia Mott (1793–1880) Abolitionist who walked the streets in the 1830s arm in arm with black women, entertained blacks at her home, and helped found the Philadelphia Female Antislavery Society. She was one of the primary organizers of the conference on women's rights at Seneca Falls, which was the effective beginning of the women's suffrage movement in the United States.

James Mulholland (1960–) A theologian, writer, and pastor with ecumenical experience. He is involved in a wide variety of social ministries.

Abraham Johannes (A.J.) Muste (1885–1967) Executive Secretary of the Fellowship of Reconciliation; leader of the Committee for Nonviolent action, which sailed boats into nuclear test zones and crossed barbed wire fences. He led peace groups and delegations across the United States, Russia, and Viet Nam.

James Naylor (1617–1660) Spiritual seeker and early Friend. He was tried for blasphemy, cruelly punished, and imprisoned.

Inazo Nitobe (1862–1933) Japanese samurai turned Quaker who devoted his life to peace. He was a professor at Tokyo University, Assistant Director General of the League of Nations, and Japan's Chief Director to the Institute of Pacific Relations.

David Niyonzima (1959–) Graduate of Kenya Highlands Bible College and George Fox University; recipient of the John Woolman Peace Award from the George Fox University's Center for Peace Learning; Coordinator of Trauma Healing and Reconciliation Services, coordinating the psychosocial intervention for traumatized people; superintendent of Burundi Yearly Meeting of Friends; Director of Evangelical Friends International, and author. He has promoted healing and rehabilitation for the victims of torture, sexual violence, and ex-combatants.

Parker J. Palmer (1939–) Author, teacher, activist, senior associate of the American Association for Higher Education, and senior adviser to the Fetzer Institute.

Sharon Daloz Parks (1942–) Former professor at Harvard Divinity School, senior research fellow at Harvard Business and Kennedy Schools, lecturer, and author. She is presently the director of Leadership for the New Commons at the Whidbey Institute in Washington State.

William Penn (1644–1718) Son of an English Admiral who became a Friend and a pacifist. He purchased land from the Delaware Native peoples for Pennsylvania, and wrote a Frame of Government for the new colony that was consistent with the philosophy of Friends and served as a model for the U.S. Constitution.

Isaac Penington (1616–1679) Writer and author born into an influential English family who risked losing his wealth and freedom by becoming a Friend. He endured religious persecution by the Puritans and wrote many of his letters and essays from English prisons.

John Punshon (1935–) British Friend, Labour Party worker, Leyton borough councillor, solicitor specializing in trade union law, and professor of Quaker Studies at Earlham School of Religion. He believes his "working class attitudes and values have enabled [him] to withstand the effects of [his] education."

Ben Richmond (1945–) Author, peace worker, past editor of *Quaker Life* magazine and a minister in the Friends Church.

Bayard Rustin (1912–1987) Lifelong pacifist and peace activist who served time in jail as a conscientious objector. He became a Civil Rights leader and was superintendent of the 1963 March on Washington, director of the A. Philip Randolph Institute, and later worked as an observer of elections in developing countries.

Douglas Steere (1901–1997) Author, professor of philosophy at Haverford College, and Quaker Observer at Vatican Council II. He was an extensive traveler to Africa, Europe, and Asia for the American Friends Service Committee.

Helen Steven (1942–) Scottish peace activist. She worked in orphanages in Vietnam, was a justice and peace worker for the Iona Community, and started both Peace House and the Scottish Centre for Nonviolence. Along with her partner Ellen Moxley, she was awarded the Gandhi International Peace Prize.

Frances Irene Tabor (1930–) Contemplative retreat leader. She grew up among Conservative Friends in the Midwest, worked with the Olney School in Ohio, and helped establish a spiritual retreat program.

Jean Toomer (1894–1967) Writer and life-long intellectual and spiritual seeker. He grew up in upper-class black Washington society, is considered part of the

"Negro Renaissance" of the 1920s, and was a close associate of Gurdjieff. He taught in the rural south, and from those experiences wrote his renowned book *Cane*.

Elizabeth Gray Vining (1902–1999) Author of children's books, religious tracts, and biographies. She sailed to Japan in 1946 at the request of the Japanese imperial family to become the personal tutor of Crown Prince Akihito.

Elizabeth Watson (1914–2006) Feminist, spiritual writer, lecturer, and workshop leader. She was committed to equality, social justice, and environmental sustainability.

John Greenleaf Whittier (1807–1892) Well-known Victorian poet, national leader in the abolitionist movement, and author of anti-slavery tracts. He once disguised himself and rushed into a burning building to save an abolitionist newspaper from an angry mob.

Lloyd Lee Wilson (1947–) A recorded minister of the gospel in the North Carolina Yearly Meeting (Conservative). Former General Secretary of the Friends General Conference, national board member of AFSC, professor of religion at Chown University, writer, and speaker on various Quaker topics.

John Woolman (1720–1772) Tailor and journalist. He is best known for his successful travels to witness nonviolently against slavery, to protect the rights of Native Americans, and to recognize the relationship between exploitive economic production and the seeds of war and injustice.

Notes

Preface

1. John Wilhelm Rowntree, "Man's Relations to God," *Essays and Addresses* (England, 1905), 397–405; *Christian Faith and Practice in the Experience of the Society of Friends* (London: London Yearly Meeting of the Religion Society of Friends, 1960), #94.

Introduction

1. Margaret Hope Bacon, *Let This Life Speak: The Legacy of Henry Joel Cadbury* (Philadelphia: University of Pennsylvania Press, 1987), 181.
2. From conversation with Margaret Benefiel about a homily delivered by James E. Keegan, SJ, at Eastern Point Retreat Center, Gloucester, Massachusetts, 2002.
3. John Yungblut, "For That Solitary Individual, An Octogenarian's Counsel on Living and Dying," Pendle Hill Pamphlet 316 (Wallingford, PA: Pendle Hill Publications, 1994), 8.
4. Everett Lewis Cattell, *The Spirit of Holiness* (Grand Rapids, MI: William B. Eerdmans Publishing Co., 1963), 54–60.
5. Bill Kreidler, "Following a Leading," from the "Seekers Journey" at Friends General Conference, 1994 (Middlebury, VT: Heron Dance Press, 2002), 37.
6. Notes from 1984 Harvard Divinity School class, "Spirituality in Historical and Developmental Perspectives," taught by Sharon Daloz Parks.
7. Rosemary Dougherty, *Group Spiritual Direction* (New York: Paulist Press, 1995), 24.
8. Alexander Solzhenitsyn, *Gulag Archipelago* (New York: Harper & Row, 1973), 168.
9. M. K. Gandhi, *Nonviolent Resistance* (New York: Schocken Books, 1951), 161.
10. From a conversation with Emily Sander in Cambridge, Massachusetts, 1993.
11. From a conversation with Kate Potter in Cape Elizabeth, Maine, 2002.
12. Walter Wink, *Engaging the Powers* (Minneapolis, MN: Fortress Press, 1992),

13. Michael H. Crosby, OFM, "The CMSM Shalom Strategy," *The Spirituality of Nonviolence* (Washington, DC: Conference of Major Superiors of Men, 1996), 29–38.
14. Parker J. Palmer, *A Hidden Wholeness* (San Francisco: Jossey-Bass, 2004), 169.
15. Elise Boulding, "Building a Culture of Peace" lecture, Bates College, October 11, 2001.
16. United Nations Educational, Scientific, and Cultural Organization Culture of Peace Program, "The Seville Statement" (Paris: UNESCO Culture of Peace Program, 1986), 1–2.
17. Walter Wink, "Can Love Save the World?," *YES! A Journal of Positive Futures* (Winter, 2002), 15.
18. From a message given by Maria Reardon at Midcoast Meeting of Friends, Damariscotta, Maine, 2002.
19. Martin Luther King, Jr., *Where Do We Go from Here: Chaos or Community?* (New York: Harper & Row, 1967), 62–63.
20. Mark 12:28–31 and Matthew 5:43.
21. Yearly Meeting of the Religious Society of Friends in Britain, *Quaker Faith and Practice* (Warwick, England: Britain Yearly Meeting, 1995), 24.03.
22. Elise Boulding, "Envisioning the Peaceful Kingdom," *Peace is the Way* (Maryknoll, NY: Orbis Books, 2000), 130–131.
23. Elise Boulding, *One Small Plot of Heaven* (Wallingford, PA: Pendle Hill Publications, 1989), 84.
24. Mark 1:15; Luke 10:9; Luke 21:31; and Luke 17:21.
25. Elise Boulding and Adam Curle, *Reflections on Peace* (Wallingford, PA: Pendle Hill Publications, 2000), 20.
26. Mark 4:26.
27. Peace Pilgrim, *Peace Pilgrim: Her Life and Work in Her Own Words* (Santa Fe, NM: Ocean Tree Books, 1983), 124.
28. Lawrence S. Apsey remembers A.J. Muste attributing these words to Emily Greene Balch in *Following the Light for Peace* (Ashland, Ohio: Kim Pathways, 1991), 244.
29. Joanna Macy, *Coming Back to Life* (Gabriola Island, BC, Canada: New Society Publishers, 1998), 23–24.
30. Elise Boulding and Adam Curle, *Reflections on Peace*, 24.
31. Thomas R. Kelly, *The Eternal Promise* (New York: Harper & Row, 1966), 57.
32. Walter Wink, "Can Love Save the World?", 15.

33. Parker Palmer, quoted in Sam M. Intrator, *Living the Questions: Essays Inspired by the Work and Life of Parker J. Palmer* (San Francisco: Jossey-Bass, 2005), xli.

34. Based on the title of Wanda Urbanska and Frank Levering's, *Nothing's Too Small to Make a Difference* (Winston-Salem, NC: John F. Blair, 2004).

35. Inspired by poet Judyth Hill's "Wage Peace," unpublished, available at www.Rockmirth.com.

36. Margaret E. Hirst, *The Quakers in Peace and War: An Account of Their Peace Principles and Practice* (London: Swarthmore Press Ltd, 1923), 481.

37. Psalm 24:3.

38. Thomas R. Kelly, *The Eternal Promise*, 57.

Chapter 1

1. Given as a message by Wendy Sanford during a Quaker Women's retreat at St. Joseph Villa Retreat Center, Cohasset, Massachusetts, 1997.

2. From conversation with Bayard Rustin's canvassing partner, Milton Kramer, Cambridge, Massachusetts, 1986.

3. From a letter to Lady Claypole in 1658, in George Fox, *The Journal of George Fox*, Rufus M. Jones, editor (Richmond, IN: Friends United Press, 1976), 321.

4. Attributed to Elwyn Brooks (E.B.) White and recalled on his death in *Newsweek*, October 14, 1985.

5. Janet Whitney, *Elizabeth Fry* (London: The British Publishers Guild, 1937), 151–152.

6. Hugh Barbour and J. William Frost, *The Quakers* (Richmond, IN: Friends United Press, 1988), 318–319.

7. June Costa, "In the Spirit of Asking and Giving" (Bethesda, MD: Shalem Newsletter, Volume 26, No. 3, Fall 2002), 1.

8. Annie Dillard, *Teaching a Stone to Talk* (New York: Harper & Row, 1982), 40–41.

9. Query suggested by Brian Drayton, 2006.

10. From the transcript of an e-mail with Darcy Drayton, 2002.

11. From the transcript of conversations with Darcy Drayton, 2002.

12. From the transcript of an e-mail with Darcy Drayton, 2002.

13. Notes from 1984 Harvard Divinity School class, "Spirituality in Historical and Developmental Perspectives," taught by Sharon Daloz Parks.

14. Hugh Barbour, *Quakers in Puritan England* (New Haven, CT: Yale University Press, 1964), 119–123.

15. Daisy Newman, *A Procession of Friends* (Richmond, IN: Friends United Press, 1972), 69.

16. Stephan G. Cary, *Speak Truth to Power: A Quaker Search for an Alternative to Violence* (Philadelphia: American Friends Service Committee, 1955), 44.

17. Margaret E. Hirst, *The Quakers in Peace and War*, 382.

18. Robert Cooney and Helen Michalowski, editors, *The Power of the People: Active Nonviolence in the United States* (Philadelphia, PA: New Society Publishers, 1987), 21.

19. Margaret E. Hirst, *The Quakers in Peace and War*, 354.

Chapter 2

1. Stephan G. Cary, *Speak Truth to Power*, 69.

2. John Woolman, *The Journal of John Woolman* (Seacaucus, NJ: The Citadel Press, 1961), 142.

3. Parker Palmer, *A Hidden Wholeness*, 181.

4. Query suggested by Benjamin Schneider, 2005.

5. Marguerite de Angeli, *Thee Hannah* (Scottdale, PA: Herald Press, 2000), 42.

6. Ibid, 97.

7. Harry Emerson Fosdick, editor, *Rufus Jones Speaks to Our Times* (New York: Macmillan, 1951), 69.

8. Elise Boulding, *One Small Plot of Heaven*, 164.

9. From a peacemaking workshop given by Frances Crow, New England Yearly Meeting, 2003.

10. A. Ruth Fry, editor, *Victories Without Violence* (Santa Fe, NM: Ocean Tree Books, 1986), 19; and Anna Pettit Broomell, *The Friendly Story Caravan* (Wallingford, PA: Pendle Hill Publications, 1935), 17–22.

11. Paul Oestreicher, "The Double Cross," in Elizabeth Cave and Ros Morley, editors, *Faith in Action: Quaker Social Testimony*, (London: Quaker Home Service, 2000), 34–35, 222.

12. Wanda Urbanska and Frank Levering, *Nothing's Too Small to Make a Difference*, 3.

13. Frank Levering and Wanda Urbanska, *Simple Living: One Couple's Search for a Better Life* (Winston-Salem, NC: John F. Blair, 1993), 265–268.

14. Douglas Steere, *Together in Solitude* (New York: Crossroad, 1982), 26–27.

15. Chuck Fager, *Without Apology* (Media, PA: Kimo Press, 1996), 87.

16. Jim Corbett, *Goatwalking: A Guide to Wildland Living* (New York: Viking Penguin, 1991).

17. From a talk by pastor Richard Foster, Renovare Conference, Portland, Maine, October 29, 2005.

18. Louis Cox, et al., editors, *Earthcare for Friends* (Burlington, VT: Earthcare Witness, 2004), 115.

19. Jamie Tarabay, "Maestro Strikes a Note of Peace: Israeli Reaches Out at West Bank School," from the Associated Press, September 11, 2002.

20. Mitchell Landsberg, "World-Class Pianist Forges a Link for Peace in the Middle East," *Los Angeles Times*, September 11, 2002.

21. William Carlos Williams, "Asphodel that Greeny Flower," *The Collected Poems of William Carlos Williams, Volume II, 1939–1962* (New York: New Directions, 1988), 318.

22. Query suggested by Benjamin Schneider, 2005.

Chapter 3

1. Kara Newell, "Quaker Profiles: Bob Philbrook," *Friends Journal*, July 2001, 32–34.

2. From conversations with Sandy Philbrook and members of Portland Friends Meeting.

3. Daniel Krieger, *Speaking of Peace*, (Santa Barbara, CA: Nuclear Age Peace Foundation), 60.

4. From the title of the book by Henri J. M. Nouwen, *The Wounded Healer* (Garden City, NY: Image Books, 1979).

5. From an interview with David Potorti, March, 2003.

6. From a talk by James Guilford, Alternatives to Violence Workshop, MCI Norfolk Prison, Norfolk, Massachusetts, 1990.

7. Henri J. M. Nouwen, *The Wounded Healer*, 20.

Chapter 4

1. Compiled by Jack Sutters, edited by Melissa K. Elliott, *Undaunted Spirits, True Stories of Quaker Service* (Philadelphia: American Friends Service Committee, 2002), 80.

2. Douglas Steere, "Mutual Irradiation: A Quaker View of Ecumenism," Pendle Hill Pamphlet 175 (Wallingford, PA: Pendle Hill Publications, 1971), 7.

3. From the foreword by Vanessa Julye in Margaret Hope Bacon, *Sarah Mapps Douglas* (Philadelphia: Quaker Press, 2003), v; Forrest G. Wood, *The Era of Reconstruction, 1863–1877* (New York: Thomas Y. Crowell Company, 1975, 48.

4. Philadelphia Yearly Meeting of the Religious Society of Friends, *Faith and Practice of Philadelphia Yearly Meeting of the Religious Society of Friends* (Philadelphia: Philadelphia Yearly Meeting of the Religious Society of Friends, 1997), 210.

5. Gerda Lerner, *The Grimke Sisters from South Carolina* (New York: Schocken Books, 1971), 1–5.

6. Ibid., 7.

7. Ibid., 8.

8. David Niyonzima and Lon Fendall, *Unlocking Horns: Forgiveness and Reconciliation in Burundi* (Newberg, OR: Barclay Press, 2001), 2–6.

9. Ibid., 8.

10. Ibid., 9.

11. Ibid.

12. Ibid., 10–11.

13. Ibid., xiv.

14. David Niyonzima, "How I Came to Be a Traveling Minister and Was Transformed in the Process," in Margery Post Abbot and Peggy Senger Parsons, editors, *Walk Worthy of Your Calling* (Richmond, IN: Friends United Press, 2004), 75.

15. Hugh Barbour et al., *Quaker Crosscurrents: Three Hundred Years of Friends in the New York Yearly Meetings* (Syracuse, NY: Syracuse University Press, 1995), 32–33; L.V. Hodgkin, *A Book of Quaker Saints* (London: Friends Home Service committee, 1972), 347–355.

Chapter 5

1. Margaret Hope Bacon, *Valiant Friend: The Life of Lucretia Mott* (New York: Walker and Company, 1980), 8–19.

2. Ibid., 140–141.

3. Ibid., 141.

4. Ibid., 142.
5. Margaret E. Hirst, *The Quakers in Peace and War*, 336; Janet Hoffman, *Some Published and Unpublished Writings of Janet Hoffman*, 1987.
6. From conversation with Martha E. Manglesdorf, 1994.
7. From an interview with Al Starr, October 2002.
8. From e-mails received from Al Starr, April 2006.
9. From conversation with Emma Hazel Harrison, November 2002.
10. Elisabeth Potts Brown and Susan Mosher Stuard, *Quaker Women Over Three Centuries* (New Brunswick, NJ: Rutgers State University, 1989), 126.
11. Mercedes M. Randall, *Improper Bostonian: Emily Greene Balch* (New York: Twayne Publishers, 1964), 132.
12. Ibid., 418–425.
13. Ibid., 406–407.
14. Kenneth Ives, *Black Quakers* (Chicago: Progressive Publisher, 1986), 41–42.
15. From conversation with Sharon Daloz Parks, December 2005.

Chapter 6

1. Mary Garmon, Margaret Benefiel, Judith Applegate, and Dortha Meredith, *Hidden in Plain Sight: Quaker Women's Writings 1650–1700* (Wallingford, PA: Pendle Hill Publications, 1996), 1.
2. Isabel Ross, *Margaret Fell: Mother of Quakerism* (York, England: William Sessions Book Trust, 1984).
3. Ibid., 285–286.
4. Margaret E. Hirst, *The Quakers in Peace and War*, 220–222.
5. Ibid., 218.
6. Henry J. Cadbury, "The Character of a Quaker," Pendle Hill Pamphlet 103 (Lebanon, PA: Sowers, 1959), 9. Originally given as the William Penn Lecture for 1959, published by special arrangement with the Young Friends Movement, Philadelphia Yearly Meeting, Philadelphia, Pennsylvania.
7. From interviews with Margaret Hope Bacon and Miriam Lust, 2003.
8. Ibid.
9. Based on an e-mail from Charlie Clements, April 2006.
10. Ibid.
11. Stephen G. Cary, *The Intrepid Quaker: One Man's Quest for Peace* (Wallingford, PA: Pendle Hill Publications, 2003), 82.

12. Ibid.
13. Linda B. Selleck, *Gentle Invaders: Quaker Women Educators and Racial Issues During the Civil War and Reconstruction* (Richmond, IN: Friends United Press, 1995), 253–255.
14. William Robertson Nicoll, "Gethsemane, the Rose Garden of God," in *The World's Great Sermons* (Volume IX), compiled by Grenville Kleiser (New York: Funk and Wagnalls Company, 1909), 211–230.
15. Margaret Hope Bacon, *Love is the Hardest Lesson* (Wallingford, PA: Pendle Hill Publications, 1999), 3.
16. Ibid., 9–12. Sophie Brown is an alias to protect the patient's privacy.
17. Ibid., 140.
18. Psalm 30:7, King James Version.
19. John Leonard, "Talking Cure?", *New York Magazine*, April 5, 1999; Bill Moyers, "Facing Truth," *PBS*, March 30, 1999.
20. Based on an e-mail from Albie Sachs, May 2006.

Glossary of Common Quaker Terms

The American Friends Service Committee (AFSC) is a Quaker service and relief organization that was awarded the Nobel Peace Prize in 1947 for its restoration work in post-war Europe.

A Clearness Committee consists of people appointed by the meeting to help an individual or group explore whether their decisions and plans are aligned with God's will for them.

The Clerk is a servant leader entrusted with facilitating a Friends Meeting for Business. There is a dynamic between the clerk and the meeting whereby the clerk draws out, discerns, and articulates the meeting's understanding of truth (sense of the meeting) during the Meeting for Business.

Continuing Revelation is the belief that God continues to speak to people today.

Discernment is the individual or group spiritual practice of coming to know God's will by prayerfully sifting through what we have heard listening within and separating it from our own frailties such as fear, pride, and ambition.

Faith and Practice is the name given to a reference book compiled by each yearly meeting that contains the collective wisdom of the community, including queries and guidelines intended to support individual and corporate faithful living.

Lamb's War is the belief that we are not to rely on outward weapons but to rely only on spiritual weapons in the faith that the Lamb of Peace will prevail (Revelation 17:12–14).

Leading is an inner sense of being called by God to undertake a particular course of action.

Meetings for Worship, in the tradition of an *unprogrammed* or *silent* meetings, are worship services where Friends gather in expectant silence, waiting upon God and the leadings of the Spirit, which may manifest in vocal messages, prayer, or silent communion. These services are not led by a pastor and do not have a prearranged program. In the tradition of *programmed* Quaker meetings, there is also the spirit of expectant waiting, but the worship is led by a pastor and there is an established order of service.

Monthly, Quarterly, and Yearly Meetings constitute the institutional structure of Friends, which is organized geographically by a calendar nomenclature (monthly, quarterly, yearly) designating the regularity of their business meetings. Local Quaker meetings are called *monthly meetings* because they meet monthly to conduct business. *Quarterly meetings* consist of several regional monthly meetings, which typically meet every three months. *Yearly meetings* are made up of several quarterly meetings, often within a state or nation, which meet together once a year.

Quaker (interchangeable with Friend) is the traditional or popular name of a member of the Religious Society of Friends. It was originally a derogatory term given by the Puritans to early Friends who sometimes "quaked" during worship or when giving public testimony.

Queries are reflection questions, usually based on Friends' testimonies, which are read and pondered for spiritual guidance by individuals and by meetings.

Spirit is the presence of God in our hearts, which illuminates truth and strengthens and guides us. It is sometimes referred to by Friends as the Guide, the Holy, the Seed, Spirit of Truth, the Inward Christ, or "that of God in everyone."

Testimonies are outward practices and attitudes that are reflections of an inward faith. Traditionally the central testimonies include simplicity, peace, integrity, community, and equality.